ONE TO GO

One to Go

JACK BERRY

with a Foreword by
SIR ALEX FERGUSON

TIMEWELL PRESS * LONDON

First published in Great Britain in 2000 by
Timewell Press Limited
8 Balham Hill, London SW12 9EA

ISBN 1 85725 155 5

Typeset by Antony Gray
Printed and bound in Great Britain by
MPG Books Ltd, Bodmin, Cornwall

I dedicate this book to our Sam

and all the other injured ex-jockeys
who have given us so much fun
and pleasure over the years

Contents

Foreword by Sir Alex Ferguson

It is my pleasure to have been asked to do the foreword for Jack's book, and it is a delight to be included in one of racing's literary chronicles.

If, like me, you have read Jack's other two books, you will know that it is tough at the bottom. This book brings to the reader the day-to-day challenges of life in the racing world. It captures the excitement, drama and heartache at the business end of a trainer's life. And it tells it like it is – no fudging the issues, everything in black and white – which to me makes it an all the more compelling read.

Although I have only been involved with the turf for a few years, I have enjoyed every minute of it. Until you snuff that early-morning air on the gallops at Cockerham, you can never truly understand the magic of preparing and looking after horses.

Without question, one of the most revealing experiences you can have is to sit in the Berrys' kitchen and listen to the countless visitors who drop in at the yard. It is more like a doctor's waiting-room, where you get all of life's 'ails'. A day that ends up in Bumbles Restaurant in the village is a day to remember.

Jack is one of racing's characters and this book expresses that clearly. Running the full gamut of emotions has been the form for him every day for countless years. You will laugh and feel sadness, but you will not be able to put the book down, and that is as good a recommendation as you will ever get.

I would just like to wish Jack a happy retirement, one that he and Jo will be able to enjoy to the full.

Introduction

This is my final year of wearing the 'I'm in charge' badge at Moss Side Racing Stables, as Alan takes over at the millennium. I am the first to admit that there should be two such badges in our yard – the other one for Jo, The Bride, who was equal partner when we started out with nothing, and still is. Whatever we have achieved, we have achieved together. As a training licence can only be held by one person, ours is in my name. Had it been possible to get a joint one, we would have done so.

I have been asked many times, 'When are you going to write another book?' So I thought, why not? My first book, *It's Tougher at the Bottom*, published by Marlborough Press in 1989, went down really well, selling twenty-one thousand copies. All five thousand copies of my second book, *A Year in Red Shirts*, my diary of 1993, were sold. I chose the title *One to Go* for this book as it gives a rundown of my activities over the past year, with a few stories from past and present thrown in.

Whilst visiting Paddy Farrell from time to time in Pindersfield Hospital, I met a young lady by the name of Kim Smith, who was also a patient there. Kim is the girlfriend of Mark Buckley, a trainer who rents a small yard in Yorkshire. On the 12 June 1999, she had a fall on the gallops. She spent three weeks in a coma in the intensive neurological unit at Leeds General Infirmary destined to be paralysed by a spinal-cord injury, her condition complicated by collapsed lungs and a chest infection. When Kim came out of her coma, she suffered a stroke which affected her speech, taste, smell and the use of her right arm. After four days, the doctors gave her little or no hope of survival. But, the battler that she is, Kim pulled through. She still has problems and spends a lot of time in hospital, but she and Mark are hopeful of having a purpose-built yard one day, so that they can continue what they set out to do. Kim has already worked as a secretary, so she could cope with office work.

A more likeable and deserving couple would be hard to find. As Kim does not qualify for racing benefits, my intention is to help the couple to fulfil their ambition by donating one pound from every copy sold of *One to Go*. When you buy this book, even if you don't read and enjoy it, you will at least have contributed something towards Mark and Kim's yard.

I need to thank some faces for the help I have received in putting it all together: Helen McWilliams, our secretary, for patience in translating my scribbles on to our word processor; Richard Smith for checking the dialogue; Nan Bibby for acting as gofer to myself and Judy Tomlinson, who beautifully typed up the copy and prepared it for my publisher. I would also like to thank all the people who have lent me photographs.

Above all, I would like to say a sincere thank you to all our owners, past and present, for sending us their horses to train. Without them, there wouldn't have been a Jack Berry.

Like Dr Shuni in the book says, sit down, relax, pour yourself a drink and enjoy the read.

Yours in sport,

JACK BERRY

1

The Speech

On the evening of 21 November 1998 our end-of-season party took place as usual at our local village hall in Cockerham. To be honest, I felt a bit nervous this year as I intended to announce that I plan to retire at the millennium and that Alan will take over the licence.

Alan is thirty-five years old. He has done spells in different yards – two years as assistant to Willie Jarvis in Newmarket, two years with Padge Berry in Ireland and another two years with Tommy Skiffington in America. Initially, I was hoping Alan would train for a couple of years in a smaller yard so when the time came we could switch roles. Alan had a look at the thirty-five-box yard that Ferdy Murphy trained from in Middleham, owned by Robert Ogden. It had recently been refurbished and was really smart. But Alan was not too keen on the place as the yard was adjacent to a main road.

Realistically, where would you match the Cockerham facilities? Alan has put as much time and effort into getting our outfit as it is as anyone, so he probably thought there would not be many better yards to train from than ours. The old man has got a bit creaky nowadays, I expect he said to himself, with his arthritis, and he is always whingeing that he spends more time travelling to and from race meetings than he does in bed, so I'll stay put.

I must say, it's great to hold records such as training the fastest hundred winners in a season and the like, but it has never been on my agenda to be the oldest man with a licence training racehorses!

Helen, our secretary, and a few more crew from our ranch, decorated the village hall with dozens of red, white and blue balloons and sets of our owners' racing colours. Julia Stephenson, caterers from Lancaster, fed us. Adrian Ross did the entertaining with his disco. And the bar kept up a roaring trade. In fact, I don't know whether to be proud or ashamed of the fact that although the bar caters for countless functions throughout the year in the hall, it is by far the busiest on our party night!

All our owners were invited to the Moss Side Racing Stables social gathering, but because some were away on holiday, some live abroad and others had prior commitments, not all could be there. I couldn't help being worried as to how the non-runners would react if they got the news of my intentions from other sources.

Alex Ferguson came to the party straight from the Sheffield game where his team had been defeated 3–1. For all that, Alex, being the sport he is, was in good form. At 9.00 p.m., just before 'feed up' time was announced, I walked on to the stage and began my speech with a joke.

'Alex Ferguson, the boss of Manchester United Football Club and a devoted Roman Catholic, went to Manchester town centre to see the Pope when he did his three-day tour of the town. Thousands of the Pope's followers gathered around Piccadilly Square to listen to the great man speak. At the very front sat a tramp in scruffy, tatty old clothes. The Pope ignored most of the flock who were pushing forward trying to shake his hand or get a close glimpse of him and walked straight up to the tramp, laid his hand on his head and spoke to him. The same thing happened the next day.

'Alex, man of the world that he is, felt a bit peeved that someone of his standing could not get close enough to His Holiness the Pope, even just to say hello, when this knight of the road repeatedly claimed his attention. For a fair-sized fee, Alex arranged to swap clothes with the tramp for the third and final day of the holy man's visit. Sure enough, the next day the Pope went straight up to the tramp (now Alex Ferguson), put his hand on his head and said, "I thought I told you yesterday and the day before to bugger off!"

'Good-evening, ladies and gentlemen, and welcome to our end-of-season party. I would like to take this opportunity to thank all our owners for sending Moss Side Racing Stables their horses to train. Without them, none of us would be here tonight celebrating yet another good year, a year which saw our yard win over a hundred races for the seventh time in the last nine years. May I also thank the jockeys, vets, farriers, accountants, contractors, suppliers and everyone else who has contributed to our excellent season, to say nothing of our loyal staff: thank you!

'To some folk, it may seem routine for us now to train over a hundred winners every season. But that is far from the case. Every winner takes plenty of getting and, as these seasons go on, winning races is certainly no easier – although we have come a long way since the 6 May 1974 when I drove our old horse-box to Wolverhampton with Fiona's Pet inside for Jo, my missus, to ride to our first victory on the Flat.

'This season we were fortunate to train three Royal Ascot winners: Rosselli, Selhurstpark Flyer and Bolshoi, a feat that has never been achieved before by a Northern yard. Rosselli, ridden by John Carroll, won the Norfolk Stakes for owners Terry and Margaret Holdcroft, for whom we had previously won the same race in 1994 with Mind Games. Chris and Antonia Deuters' Selhurstpark Flyer ('George' as we all affectionately know him) bravely won the Wokingham for the second year running, ridden by the season's top apprentice, Carl Lowther. Bolshoi, also ridden by Carl Lowther, won the Group 2 King's Stand Stakes for his owner-breeders Trish and David Brown. In addition to winning the King's Stand, Bolshoi also won the Group 2 Temple Stakes at Sandown. Although we have run horses in many parts of the world, Bolshoi was our first contender in the Breeders' Cup at Churchill Downs where he ran a gallant race to finish a close seventh.

'I am proud to say that two of our apprentices, Paul Fessey and Carl Lowther, rode out their allowances this season, which is a remarkable feat as only a handful of youngsters have done that in the North in all the years I have worked in racing. In addition, Paul Roberts would also have lost his right to claim had he not had the misfortune to need an operation on his back which kept him out of the saddle for three months. Among our other beginners, Paul Bradley rode fifteen winners, Iona Wands rode three winners, Beverley Kendal got off the mark and Mette Hanssen almost did, getting placed several times.

'It is also rewarding that four of this year's leading apprentices, Alan Daly, Adrian Nicholls, Derek McGaffin and Neil Pollard, all had a spell working at Moss Side, which pays its own compliment to the standard of riding we have in the yard.

The famous five in 1998: Iona Wands, Carl Lowther, Paul Roberts,
Paul Fessey and Paul Bradley

'When Joe Heler, our stable sponsor for the last three years, initially sponsored the yard, it gave our owners the chance to recover the VAT on their training fees at a very difficult time in racing. We are extremely grateful to him. Next year, we have a change of sponsor, and we are currently negotiating a deal with Saab, who already sponsor the yards of Henry Cecil and Linda Ramsden.

'Carl Lowther has left our employment to ride as first jockey to Les Eyre. Flash, our head-man of nine years, is to marry our secretary, Helen, in three days' time. I am sure everyone would like to wish them both well. To commemorate the occasion we have named a two-year-old filly Helen's Wedding.

'I don't intend going on spouting for much longer but this is as good a time as any to inform you that this coming season will be my last as trainer at the yard; Alan will take over the licence at the end of next season. After training for thirty years, I consider it high time a younger person took hold of the reins.

'With the help of you all, and others before you, we have achieved some memorable feats. To highlight just a few:

* winning the Ayr Gold Cup with So Careful in 1988
* achieving the Royal Ascot treble this year
* training at least one two-year-old winner on every Flat course in Britain
* holding the record for the fastest fifty and the fastest hundred winners in a season
* being the leading yard numerically on three different occasions
* being the leading yard in the North nearly every year for the past one and a half decades
* training some good horses for some nice people!

'All good stuff. And I could go on. Jo and I have so much to be thankful for and it will be a lot to give up. However, we will still be at the yard for some time, only in a less high-profile role. We want the stables to carry on the good work under Alan for many years to come, and all of you, owners and staff, to continue to be a crucial part of it. But before I hand over the reins to Alan, I would dearly love to train a Group 1 winner. With your help, we will be flat out to achieve that goal next season.

'Thank you all for coming tonight and enjoy yourselves!'

After singing (or, some would say, strangling) 'The Jolly Farmer', I left the stage and we all ate, drank, danced and had a great night.

Although no gentlemen of the press were present, by Monday they had got a whiff of my retirement plans and the news made front-page headlines in the *Racing Post* and a mention in most other papers. The following day, when I was on my way to one of my now rare visits to Market Rasen, three radio stations and lots of pressmen rang up for confirmation of my intentions and some words. An interview with Doug Fraser for the Racing Channel followed when I arrived at the racecourse, where our runner Smolensk was withdrawn minutes before the race because of heavy going caused by overnight rain. At Market Rasen people were dazed by the news, many finding it hard to believe. Some commiserated with me, others were full of congratulations. I was told that when Lambourn trainer Mick Channon heard, he said straightaway, 'Thank f**k for that. We might get a chance to train a few two-year-old winners now!' It must have been said tongue-in-cheek as Mick is a great trainer, a good pal and does exceptionally well with his youngsters.

2

Pleasant Days

The last Saturday in November 1998, Jo and I were invited to a most enjoyable day's jump-racing at Haydock Park by the Horserace Betting Levy Board chairman, Robert Hughes, and his chief executive, Rodney Brack. Also present was Home Office minister George Howarth and the wives of the three men. I don't know if Rodney thought we were big punters when he sent out our invitations, but we're not. However, I did have a few pounds with the Tote credit office that day on Venetia Williams's Teeton Mill who won the Hennessy at Newbury.

The following Thursday, Go Racing in Yorkshire held their annual luncheon at the Ripon Spa Hotel, where trophies sponsored by Thomson Local Directories were presented for the Flat season's leading trainer and jockey. The trophies had been displayed at all nine of the county's courses, with an update on the jockeys' and trainers' positions throughout the season.

Kevin Darley won the jockey's award for the second year running. Our yard, with twenty-seven Yorkshire winners, won the beautiful pewter trophy of a horse and jockey, which Jo and I were grateful and delighted to receive. Christopher Tetley of Go Racing in Yorkshire, Tote chairman Peter Jones and John Sexton, president of the Horserace Writers' and Photographers' Association, were the speakers.

We ate succulent roast sirloin of beef with Yorkshire pudding, followed by hot apple pie with cheese, a desert I have not eaten since leaving Yorkshire some twenty-seven years ago. Sir Clement Freud, racing's food connoisseur, would have loved it! Mind you, there was no sign of my old pal and fellow trainer, Mick Easterby. Probably a good job, too. I'm told that he once went out to dinner at a flash restaurant in Yorkshire and the maître d'hôtel put screens up to separate him from the other diners.

Now that I am of an age to qualify, I received an invitation to the Christmas party for the over-60s at our local village hall, which was good fun.

On 7 December, Jo and I travelled to London for the 1998 Horserace Writers' and Photographers' Association's Derby Awards Luncheon at the Royal Lancaster Hotel, which is a gathering of most of the personalities of racing. Geoff Snook from Barry Hill's yard and Michael Leaman, who works for Clive Brittain's outfit, jointly took the stable-staff awards. Owner of the Year went to the Summit Partnership whose Earth Summit won the Grand National. The real McCoy, Tony, won the honour for being top jump jockey. Kieren Fallon, who rode out of his skin all season, took the Flat jockey's award for the second year running.

Claude Duval was voted Journalist of the Year and gave a very long but entertaining speech. The legendary Martin Pipe won the National Hunt title for the fifth time (no less), beating Peter Easterby's joint record of four past awards. Saeed bin Suroor had plenty to celebrate, being the International and Home Trainer of the Year (yours truly had been the grateful recipient of the latter title in 1990). Finally the 'David Bailey of the Year' went to Alec Russell.

If I said I saw this fellow hitchhiking and I gave him a lift, I would be telling untruths, but my old mate Bob Champion had come by train from Newmarket for the Derby Awards. As Jo and I had to go to the Newmarket Sales after the lunch and as Bob knew the best route out of London, I persuaded him to drive our car. At the sales, Alex Ferguson's Queensland Star was bought by Charlie Gordon-Watson for twenty-five thousand guineas to race in America. I was sorry to lose him, but with his high rating he could be hard to place as a three-year-old. Lord Mostyn's Conwy Lodge was sold for ten thousand guineas to continue his career in Dubai.

With this particular event being so close to Christmas, every year I help Serena Oxley, the southern-based Injured Jockeys almoner, to sell Injured Jockeys Fund Christmas cards in the foyer near the bar and restaurant. The total for the half-hour stint amounted to three hundred and forty-eight pounds, plus fifteen Irish punts, which beat our previous record by fifty pounds. I might add that the sale of Injured Jockeys Fund Christmas cards is the charity's biggest source of income.

We stayed overnight at our second home, Gerry and Bridget Blum's. The night was memorable in that I beat Mrs Blum at Jenga for the first time ever and went to bed very pleased with myself.

Next day our travelling head-man, John Murray, brought Bolshoi down in our horse-box to headquarters for the horse's first leg of his trip to run in the $1,380,000 Sprinter's Stakes at Nakayama in Japan on 20 December. As Bolshoi had won the Temple Stakes at Sandown and the King's Stand Stakes at Royal Ascot, his owners thought, quite rightly, they would let him take his chance, as there are not too many good sprinters in Japan. In addition, he would collect $72,000 even for finishing fifth. Rachel Hume, the horse's groom, and John travelled with Bolshoi. My missus drove the box back home as it didn't make sense leaving it at Newmarket for a couple of weeks waiting for the horse to return.

That evening, I attended the 228th annual Gymcrack Club Dinner. Aziz Merza, representative of His Highness Sheikh Ahmed bin Rashid al Maktoum, owner of Gymcrack winner Josr Algarhoud, made the traditional Gymcrack speech. Peter Savill, chairman of the British Horserace Board spoke on the subject of racing's finances. In the following morning's *Racing Post*, his comments came in for harsh criticism from the bookmakers, from whom he thought racing should be getting more money.

Lambourn trainer Richard Phillips had everyone howling with laughter as he impersonated a number of racing personalities. As you can see from the seating-plan, I was in good company.

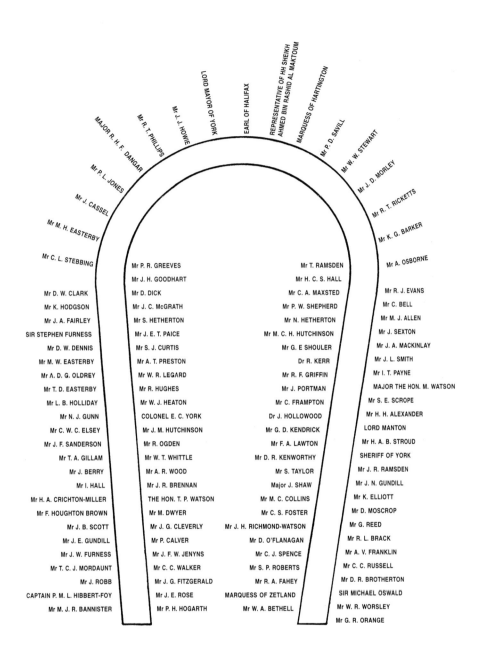

LORD MAYOR OF YORK
EARL OF HALIFAX
REPRESENTATIVE OF HH SHEIKH AHMED BIN RASHID AL MAKTOUM
MARQUESS OF HARTINGTON
Mr J. J. HOWIE
Mr R. T. PHILLIPS
Mr P. D. SAVILL
MAJOR R. H. F. DANGAR
Mr W. W. STEWART
Mr P. L. JONES
Mr J. D. MORLEY
Mr J. CASSEL
Mr R. T. RICKETTS
Mr M. H. EASTERBY
Mr K. G. BARKER
Mr C. L. STEBBING
Mr A. OSBORNE

Mr D. W. CLARK	Mr P. R. GREEVES	Mr T. RAMSDEN	Mr R. J. EVANS
	Mr J. H. GOODHART	Mr H. C. S. HALL	Mr C. BELL
Mr K. HODGSON	Mr D. DICK	Mr C. A. MAXSTED	Mr M. J. ALLEN
Mr J. A. FAIRLEY	Mr J. C. McGRATH	Mr P. W. SHEPHERD	Mr J. SEXTON
SIR STEPHEN FURNESS	Mr S. HETHERTON	Mr N. HETHERTON	Mr J. A. MACKINLAY
Mr D. W. DENNIS	Mr J. E. T. PAICE	Mr M. C. H. HUTCHINSON	Mr J. L. SMITH
Mr M. W. EASTERBY	Mr S. J. CURTIS	Mr G. E SHOULER	Mr I. T. PAYNE
Mr A. D. G. OLDREY	Mr A. T. PRESTON	Dr R. KERR	MAJOR THE HON. M. WATSON
Mr T. D. EASTERBY	Mr W. R. LEGARD	Mr R. F. GRIFFIN	Mr S. E. SCROPE
Mr L. B. HOLLIDAY	Mr R. HUGHES	Mr J. PORTMAN	Mr H. H. ALEXANDER
Mr N. J. GUNN	Mr W. J. HEATON	Mr C. FRAMPTON	LORD MANTON
Mr C. W. C. ELSEY	COLONEL E. C. YORK	Dr J. HOLLOWOOD	Mr H. A. B. STROUD
Mr J. F. SANDERSON	Mr J. M. HUTCHINSON	Mr G. D. KENDRICK	SHERIFF OF YORK
Mr T. A. GILLAM	Mr R. OGDEN	Mr F. A. LAWTON	Mr J. R. RAMSDEN
Mr J. BERRY	Mr W. T. WHITTLE	Mr D. R. KENWORTHY	Mr J. N. GUNDILL
Mr I. HALL	Mr A. R. WOOD	Mr S. TAYLOR	Mr K. ELLIOTT
Mr H. A. CRICHTON-MILLER	Mr J. R. BRENNAN	Major J. SHAW	Mr D. MOSCROP
Mr F. HOUGHTON BROWN	THE HON. T. P. WATSON	Mr M. C. COLLINS	Mr G. REED
Mr J. B. SCOTT	Mr M. DWYER	Mr C. S. FOSTER	Mr R. L. BRACK
Mr J. E. GUNDILL	Mr J. G. CLEVERLY	Mr J. H. RICHMOND-WATSON	Mr A. V. FRANKLIN
Mr J. W. FURNESS	Mr P. CALVER	Mr D. O'FLANAGAN	Mr C. C. RUSSELL
Mr T. C. J. MORDAUNT	Mr J. F. W. JENYNS	Mr C. J. SPENCE	Mr D. R. BROTHERTON
Mr J. ROBB	Mr C. C. WALKER	Mr S. P. ROBERTS	SIR MICHAEL OSWALD
CAPTAIN P. M. L. HIBBERT-FOY	Mr J. G. FITZGERALD	Mr R. A. FAHEY	Mr W. R. WORSLEY
Mr M. J. R. BANNISTER	Mr J. E. ROSE	MARQUESS OF ZETLAND	Mr G. R. ORANGE
	Mr P. H. HOGARTH	Mr W. A. BETHELL	

Seating plan for 228th annual
Gymcrack Club Dinner – 7 December 1998

21

3

The Jumpers

In mid-December we ran our full National Hunt string of three at Doncaster. Carlisle Banditos finished third in the three-mile novice chase. Amlwch, owned and bred by Lord Mostyn, put up a sound display of jumping to win the two-mile novice chase on his first attempt over fences, ridden, like The Bandit, by my pal Benny Powell's son, Brendan. In the two-mile feature handicap chase, Smolensk, ridden by Mr Sam Stronge on his first outing for two hundred days, hacked up to win by sixteen lengths.

As a young amateur, Sam rode Smolensk last season at Hereford to his first win in professional company. Luckily for Sam, Tony McCoy, who had originally been booked, unfortunately suffered a fall and was injured. Smolensk must have a liking for Hereford, as on his previous race at the track, ridden by Shane Kelly, he broke the track record for the two-mile chase which had stood for twenty-four years.

Carlisle Banditos, who was bred by Sheila and Brendan Powell, was appropriately christened following a steward's inquiry at Carlisle when our Frisky Miss, ridden by Paul Roberts, won and was disqualified. According to the *Raceform Notebook*: 'Frisky Miss chased the leaders, switched over a furlong out, slightly nudged the runner-up when going through and was then continuously leant on by the third.' Undeterred, she led a furlong out and scrambled home to score by the narrowest of margins. She later lost the race in the stewards' room and her rider was suspended for four days.

On this occasion the punishment did not fit the crime. My view was that if the stewards had thrown the filly out for the slight nudge, then fair enough. But they didn't. Anthony Gillam, the stipendary steward, attempted to tell me later that the infringement with Frisky Miss took place just after the filly had travelled a furlong from the start. No way should Frisky Miss have been disqualified on that account. Needless to say the officials knew I wasn't suited and Paul honestly didn't (and still doesn't) know what he had done wrong. You can't cook with cold fat, you have to heat it up!

Stipes often over-react, confuse and terrorise the kids. By making the bullets for the stewards, they put words into the apprentices' mouths. At times you wonder if they are in the right job – they'd be better employed out haunting houses. Often the youngsters become defence-less and crumble. Then they will say anything just to get out of the officials' clutches. I am not a greedy person, a poor sport or one to throw the toys out of the pram when things don't suit. However, in my book, right is right, and if I am right, I'm like a Jack Russell with a rat. I won't let it go. That was an unfair verdict and to commemorate it I came up with the name Carlisle Banditos. If Weatherbys had not allowed the name, I was prepared to call him 'Tealeaf' or 'Removalist'. But, at the end of the day, I can't grumble about my lot. There isn't a suitcase large enough to hold all the good memories that I have from racing.

Some years back, jockey Roy Swindlehurst, Jo, some of our appren-tices and I used to go over to the Isle of Man three or four times a year to ride in the races. Meetings were held at Great Meadow and the weights were about the same as on the mainland. Except for Roy and a couple of the kids, the rest of us struggled to do the weight on the Flat.

Mrs Paddy Rigall, whom everyone called Dizzy, a very fussy woman who flapped like hell, ran the show. She hated us putting up over-weight. We all used to stay in her big house the night before racing. She had a small sauna upstairs and would make us go in to lose weight, or so she thought. We had no chance of doing under nine stone seven, so we used to go into one of our bedrooms, play cards and have a smoke.

If we couldn't get on the scheduled flight, Dizzy used to send a plane over to pick us up from Blackpool airport. We got paid well, with riding fees and expenses, but she made us work for it. We helped put hurdles up for the jump race (the rest were Flat races) and throw a bit of sand around the very sharp hairpin bends to stop horses slipping, as the going was always like concrete.

Our team rode quite a few winners there. One year, in the early 1970s, I came second in the Manx Derby. You'll never guess who rode the winner – Malton trainer Jimmy Fitzgerald. The fat sod put up two stone overweight. As we were walking around at the gate, noticing that Jimmy had his knees under his chin, I said to him, 'I know this is only a flat race, mate, but you're riding two holes shorter than Lester Piggott. Can't you let your jerks down?'

'They're on the last hole. I borrowed this saddle from Tommy Skiffington [the American jockey who rode for Jimmy at the time]. Do me a big favour, Jack, and swap me leathers. I won't make it to the first bend before I fall off.'

'Go on,' I said. 'Seeing it's you, I will.'

Dizzy's husband, Colonel Rigall, was confined to a wheelchair, but he acted as Clerk of the Course on racedays. He used to run around in a clapped-out pick-up that was always coughing and spluttering. I think he ran it on paraffin as clouds of smoke used to gush out of the exhaust pipe when he stepped on the gas. What a noise it made, and it stank something awful. The old boy shouted instructions to us course-builders from the cab. The colonel used to drive like hell, and with him being a bit dicky, he couldn't always get his foot to the brakes quick enough, and frequently drove through a hedge.

Dizzy was always getting at the colonel, and no matter what he told us, she would always want it done differently. Once, when we put up the weighing-room, which was a tent about ten foot by ten foot, in the makeshift paddock, one of the part-time workers at the course helped us to rig the old-fashioned scales (which were the type coal merchants used for weighing their fuel) to make them weigh about ten pounds light. Some of the local riders complained the scales were weighing wrong. One of the women stewards, a mountain of a lady who must have weighed about two and a half hundredweight, was invited by Dizzy to try them. When she got on the scales she must have been pleased with what she saw, as she said, 'They seem about right to me, Dizzy!'

Everything was chaos there, and the races seldom got off on time. It's a good job that senior stipendary steward Captain Hibbert-Foy didn't officiate on the Isle of Man, as there aren't many meetings that he attends in Britain these days when at least one jockey doesn't get a few days' holiday. Possibly some of these military types have to keep everyone on their toes. As there is no war on, they miss the action and reading books is not enough to satify them. Years ago, we had a highly bred sheepdog, but we didn't have any sheep. Dick, the dog, was so desperate for some work that the silly bugger used to round up the chickens and drive them all over the yard. The captain would have had a field-day at Great Meadow. But there is one thing for certain, we had a lot of fun. There was a great social gathering in the bar tent after racing, and it was there Dizzy coughed up our fees, expenses and percentages.

You may believe that there are some sharp people in racing, but you probably think that I've been around long enough to know a con-man when I see one. Just before lunch today – Monday, 14 December 1998 – I was sitting in the kitchen when The Bride let this fellow into the house. Although I had never seen him in my life before, he was all over me like a rash, with his arm stretched out to shake my hand. He was more full of bollocks than Linford Christie's underpants.

'Jack,' he says, 'I have come all the way over from Carlisle to do your portrait.'

'You had no need to,' I said, 'I've had enough of them done.'

'That's great. Keep looking to the front. Brilliant. Brilliant,' he says, looking very sincere. 'This will be spectacular! I am doing it in colour and I am only charging you forty-five pounds.'

Money isn't easy to get off a Yorkshireman unless it's earned. Following a debate, and given the fact that he had already started, he agreed to forty pounds and finished in about twenty minutes. At the same time, our housekeeper Joanna, who grafts like stink for four pounds twenty an hour, is dashing round like a mad thing to justify her wages. The masterpiece is overleaf.

Hasn't he got some bits! If he sees his crap in here he will probably want copyright too, as Colin Turner did when he had been commissioned by Red Mills Horse Feeds to take a photo of our three Royal Ascot winners for their Christmas calendar. Colin sent me a bill for twenty-five pounds for the copyright when we printed the photo on this

JB's portrait

year's Christmas cards, which he must have seen somewhere. Red Mills had already given us permission to use it. I wonder if Colin and the Carlisle version of Leonardo da Vinci are related?

At the moment we are in the process of buying two new horse-boxes. The older boxes were purchased in good faith as being capable of transporting four horses. But when four horses are loaded and the man from the Ministry of Transport pulls them up to weigh them on the way in or out of race meetings, he says the boxes are overweight. It's like treading through a minefield, keeping in line with the law. Rules and regulations, nowadays! On one occasion when we just had two horses in the front stalls we were told that there was too much weight on the front axle. Steve, the driver, moved one of the horses into the rear stalls. 'You are in order now, but I will still have to put my report in. You should be all right,' the inspector told Steve. We still got fined. Typical! I'm only doing my job. These people have no heartbeat. Reasoning with them does as much good as tits on a bull.

It's not too often one sees the 'travelling' type of vehicle pulled in to be checked – probably because they're usually owned by Messrs Smith of no fixed abode; if you think it's difficult getting money out of a Yorkshireman, it's impossible from those tinker types. A few years ago we were fined a total of two thousand six hundred pounds for seventeen offences – drivers driving over their allotted time through hold-ups in the traffic, or drivers not taking their breaks when they should, etc. Seventeen offences sounds a lot but when one considers three horse-boxes chasing up and down the country virtually every day in summer, clocking up in the region of two hundred thousand miles a year, seventeen minor offences doesn't seem too bad.

Our small fleet makes me feel like the Eddie Stobart of Cockerham. Please remember when you see the flash, patriotic red, white and blue spanking new boxes bowling along the motorway or stuck in the inevitable traffic jams, we have not won the lottery. We have been forced into buying them to keep within the law. When the painter came down to the yard the other day to price up the artwork, his fee for painting one horse on either side of each box was more than I have spent on buying some real horses.

4

It's Not All Plain Sailing

The results from the meeting at Wolverhamton on Wednesday, 16 December, made me feel rather chuffed with myself as our well-bred three-year-old filly Yanomani, owned by the Bearstone Stud, had finally won her maiden, following six fruitless attempts, making her quite valuable to breed from.

My feeling of hero was soon turned to zero by a reversed-charge call at 6.45 on Friday morning from David Brown at the racecourse stables at Nakayama in Japan. The previous day Rachel had rung from Japan saying that they had had an earth tremor and that it was the most frightening thing that she had ever experienced. Now sensing that something was amiss, I cautiously asked how Bolshoi was.

'Not good, I'm afraid,' replied David.

'Why? What's wrong, mate?'

'Bolshoi has fractured his near-fore cannon-bone!'

I was too frightened to ask if Bolshoi was still alive, but listened while David explained that Michael Roberts rode our horse on the racecourse that morning and suspected nothing until Bolshoi faltered at the end of his work when being pulled up. As John and Rachel led the horse back to the yard, he was walking short. By the time they got back to the stables, Bolshoi was severely lame and in pain. X-rays showed the leg to have a four-inch vertical crack up the cannon-bone.

As the Browns are very good friends of the Deuters, my first phonecall that morning was to Chris and Antonia, letting them know what an ugly hand the Browns had been dealt. Antonia reminded that it was exactly a year since Salamanca, a really sharp two-year-old we trained for the Deuters, had died of colic at the Browns' stud.

During the day, David rang me back to tell me that the vets had

28

inserted six screws in Bolshoi's leg. The operation went very well and the horse had come round all right from the anaesthetic but would have to stay in Japan for four to six weeks and Rachel would need to stay with him. By the time she gets home she will probably be speaking Japanese.

There's more, as Jimmy Crickett would say. We had a phonecall, just before 9 p.m., informing us that Bob, our retired handyman/gardener, had died.

By December, the majority of our older horses have gone to various livery yards all over the country, preferably where there are some hills to walk up for one and a half hours a day for four to six weeks. Then they are brought back to Cockerham all muscled-up, ready to start cantering. This gives the horses a nice change of scenery and us more time to concentrate on getting the yearlings educated and ready to race. At the present, we only have a few all-weather horses and three jumpers around, which are great to lead the youngsters with.

Most of our yearlings are now ridden away and are hacking in figures of eight, cantering in pairs or small bunches. We have had a lot of rain in this neck of the woods during the winter. Les Dawson used to say, 'It gets so wet in Lancashire they have lifeboat practice on the buses!' This year is the wettest I can remember. On occasions it curtailed the youngsters' preparation. However, on a nice day, they seem as forward as in other years. Mind you, if we did not like them at this stage, it would be a bad job.

Today, 22 December, will always be a day to remember for our apprentice Mette Hanssen, who rode her first winner on Mary Jane at Southwell. It was very foggy and we only saw the last two furlongs. Mette was riding a good race with half a furlong to go when she gratefully patted the filly's neck, having mistaken the winning-post. Thankfully, Mary Jane knew where it was and galloped right to the line to win by one and a quarter lengths.

It just shows how poor the market was for second-hand racehorses this year, as we were able to buy back the good-looking Mary Jane, already the winner of two races, at the November Sales for just sixteen hundred guineas, mainly for our apprentices to get a bit of race practice on. The filly's success gave our yard its last Flat win of the season, bringing the final score to one hundred and ten, which puts the yard once again in front for winners in the North and second numerically in the country, just one winner behind John Dunlop. No better man to be second to than John!

On Sunday, Jo and I are going for our annual three-week holiday in Barbados, where we rent a villa on the Sandy Lane estate with Newmarket trainer Michael Jarvis, his missus Gay and daughter Jackie. The villa belongs to John Moreton who owned Twin Oaks, trained by the late Gordon Richards. Before we leave it is always hectic getting everything finalised. My dogs know we are going away and are under my feet more than ever at the moment! I am happy with the yearlings and the few all-weather horses and I could not be more pleased with the jumpers. They are great.

Last night we were out for dinner at Ruth and John Barrett's house. They owned Our Fan, the horse that gave us our record-breaking one hundredth winner on 17 July 1991. This afternoon we have been to our local restaurant, Bumbles, for a Christmas lunch with one of our owners, Neil Smith. Afterwards, Jo dragged me shopping in Garstang – thankfully only for groceries this time. As we were out in her car, I didn't have any option, but I did have my ears back. If there was a competition for shoppers in the Olympics then my missus would be on the short-list to represent Britain.

It's Bob's funeral tomorrow; these days I seem to attend a lot more funerals than christenings. I worry about Bob's wife, Gladys. Every Sunday for the last three years, when I've been at home, I have taken her to the nursing home to see Bob. When I couldn't go, Alan did the honours. For the past year or so Bob has not known what day it was, with him suffering from that awful Alzheimer's Disease. When one sees the state some old people end up in, one realises there is a lot to be said for putting sick and worn-out old horses down; there is no way one would let an animal suffer like poor old Bob did.

At least Bolshoi is well on the mend. John Murray came back from Japan with the horse's X-rays to show me today. John said the vets were absolutely brilliant and what a good job they did on Bolshoi in the Miho

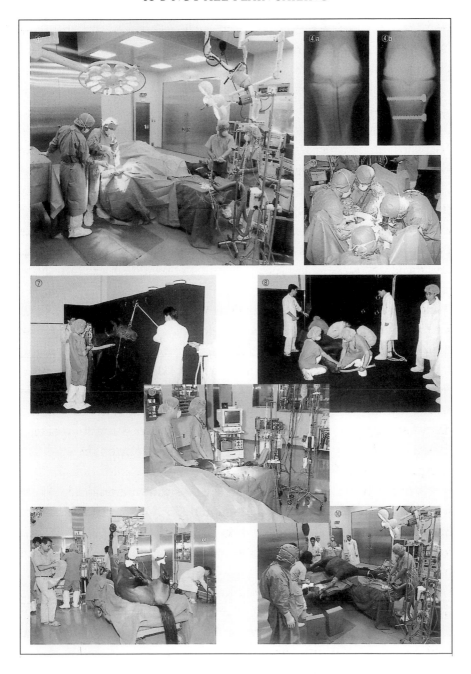

Miho Training Center and Racehorse Hospital

Racehorse Hospital, where the facilities were as good as in any hospital. The racecourse authorities were very good to our staff and horse, which is greatly appreciated when one's in a foreign country.

We have no runners on Boxing Day, but I am looking forward to my day's racing at Wetherby, where I rode my first winner on Sasra Gri in 1957. Jo and I are meeting with former trainer Walter Wharton and his wife Betty, along with John and Anne Walmsley, whom we are going to have dinner with after racing. The Walmsley family were formidable show-jumpers when I was a lad. My grandad bought me my first pony from John's dad, Billy.

Weather permitting, we run Amlwch and The Bandit (Carlisle Banditos) at Carlisle's Christmas meeting. Unfortunately, with the holiday, I won't be there to see them perform. The Bandit should raise a few eyebrows with the locals, although he won't run if the going gets heavy, something that never bothered the late jump trainer W. A. Stephenson, who used to say, 'I never worry about the going – it's the coming back that bothers me.'

Looking at the Carlisle list of officials I see my old pal Graham McMillan is acting as steward. Graham loves a bit of fun and we had plenty of that when we were both riding for the Scottish trainer, Pat Ferris, in the sixties. Another friendly face on the panel is Arthur Eubank's, while yet another mate, Phil Tuck, is steward's secretary.

Phil was always a good laugh when he was riding and could imitate Gordon Richards as well as Richard Phillips does his subjects today. John Leach is the starter. He and I rode jumpers for Harry Bell and were quite friendly then, although we seem to have drifted apart. In fact, I have known John to be a bit hostile towards me in his official role. I hope that The Bandit is facing the right way when the tape goes up!

It was a sad affair at the crematorium seeing Bob off. Poor old Gladys wasn't with it at all. I told Gladys that I would pick her up for her dinner on Christmas Day, in accordance with tradition, but she rang up at 1.30 in the morning on Christmas Day to tell me I was late. She couldn't sleep and was confused. I quietly suggested she should go back to bed and told her I would pick her up at 1 p.m. As it happened, we hadn't retired for the night as we had some friends in after Midnight Mass. Our vicar, Roger, did not take the service this year as he had to go to another church that he is in charge of. Someone must have given the ringer vicar a bung to be quick as the sermon was the shortest I can remember.

On Christmas Day, all our staff who work and can't get home have their Christmas lunch with us in our house. I can assure you that no one felt like working evening stables after Jo had stuffed us all with food and drink.

It poured with rain all day at Wetherby races but for all that it was a great meeting with good racing. The company and the food at the Walmsleys' was terrific and tomorrow we are flying off to Barbados. Yee–Hah!

5

A Nice Break

You would have though we had seen enough rain at Wetherby, but when we reached Barbados airport it was absolutely pouring down. As we made our way to the villa, the flooding was two feet deep on some roads.

The next day the Jarvises and the Berrys were laid out on sunbeds round the pool reading. Mine was Jenny Pitman's autobiography, which I though was great. To be successful one needs the rub of the green or the bounce of the ball, but the determination Jenny Pitman has shown is an example to all potential lady trainers or indeed ladies keen to get

The Jarvises and Berrys in Barbados

on in any walk of life. There is no doubt that women do have a lot more to prove to be successful in racing. Having said that, young Venetia Williams is some operator who is really putting the fairer sex on the training map, not only with Teeton Mill, who recently won the Hennessy and the King George, but with all her horses, as her record of twenty-nine per cent winners to runners at the time of writing shows. She is outstanding. I have suggested in the past that female riders should claim a five-pound allowance from males, but this lady trainer is so good at her job other jump trainers probably think her horses should carry a five-pound penalty.

Here in Barbados, Liz Dearn is a lady of note. Liz trained three of the seven winners on Saturday at the opening meet at Garrison Savannah, to which Jo and I were invited by the Barbados Racing Club. Like last year, I was asked to judge the best-turned-out horse in the feature race. In the great heat there was one old stablehand who was wearing a big pair of Wellington boots with one of the soles flapping as he walked. I am nearly certain he was there last year with the very same boots on. As the fellow looked in desperate need of a blacksmith – and, to be fair, the horses looked much the same – I gave his charge my vote, so let's hope he puts the Barbadian dollars to good use.

Through coming here over the years we are quite friendly with Liz Dearn. Four years ago Liz gave me a pit bull terrier pup as a guard dog for home. Unfortunately, we couldn't get him over to England, as the authorities have banned the importation of such breeds, which now have to be castrated, micro-chipped and tattooed in Britain.

Barbados is often called Newmarket-by-Sea because so many racing people holiday there. This year was no exception and we saw all the regulars. I always pay a visit to former Newmarket trainer Bill Marshall, who, I am glad to report, is still going strong and turning out winners in his eighties.

Jo and I called to see John Hales, the producer of the Teletubbies and owner of One Man. I arranged to pick him up at his beach house to go to see Amlwch and Carlisle Banditos in action from Carlisle on SIS at Federals, the bookies in Bridgetown. Unfortunately, it was a wasted journey as Carlisle was abandoned due to water-logging.

We later met up with the Jarvises and went to ex-trainer Franny Lee's barbecue. This is the third year we have holidayed with Michael, Gay and Jackie and we all get on like a house on fire. What a head I woke up with next morning! I hope there is truth in the words on the plaque screwed on the front door of our villa 'Allegria': 'God does not from our allotted life-span deduct the time spent drinking.'

This time last year Gordon Richards, John Hales and I were discussing One Man on the beach. Gordon said to John, 'Listen to what that man says, John. He knows a lot about a horse's speed and he knows a bit about jumpers – he rode enough of them.'

To be honest, I felt a bit humble and deeply honoured to think a trainer of the calibre of Gordon and the owner of one of the best chasers in Britain could be interested in what I thought about their great horse.

I more or less said then what I had said when I was guest speaker at a charity racing do in Edinburgh, when I was asked what I thought would win the Cheltenham Gold Cup. My view was that if the Gold Cup was run at two and a half miles instead of three and a quarter, One Man would win. Nothing had been travelling better three fences out in his previous attempts in the Gold Cup. One Man was a very good horse but the only way he would get the trip in the Gold Cup was in a horse-box. Therefore I would love to see him run in the two-mile Queen Mother's Champion Chase.

Not everyone agreed. One knowledgeable punter said, 'If One Man runs in the Queen Mother, I will give you 20–1 against him winning.' 'That's a good price. Could I have twenty pounds on him,' I asked. 'No problem,' he said in front of one hundred and forty witnesses. I have seen the man since, when racing in Scotland, and reminded him of One Man's victory in the Queen Mother. There is no need for Customs and Excise to get excited about collecting the levy, as I am still waiting to get weighed-in!

The talk with John and Gordon on their favourite subject came like music to their ears. But what a tragedy for the lovely grey horse, on his next run after winning the Queen Mother Chase, when he broke a leg at Aintree.

On New Year's Eve, John Hales invited Jo and me to their family party at the famous Mullins Bar, which, like the villa we are staying in, is owned by John Moreton. To mix a bit of business with pleasure John, Walter Gott and Steve Lee each became the proud owners of a leg in a two-year-old colt we bought in Ireland, by Nicolotte, which is to be named Four Men and will race in John's One Man colours.

On our last night in Barbados, Willie Carson, Terry Holdcroft, Rodney Meredith, myself and our wives went for a meal to Tam's Wok in Holetown and, as always, the food was first-class. Like most Chinese, Tam loves racing. Apart from being an award-winning cook, Tam is a highly skilled acupuncturist. He sorted out a trapped nerve in my shoulder which was giving me a bit of aggravation. Willie Carson suffers a lot of pain with his back, so I put him in for some treatment the following morning, which must have done him good as I later saw him in a cooking programme on TV looking in great form.

We had a brilliant night. You can imagine the subject of conversation with Tam, who joined us after his kitchen chores. Needless to say we were by far the latest to leave the restaurant.

During the evening, I reminded Willie of a bet he had had with Joe Heler, owner-breeder of our good filly, My Melody Parkes, some four years ago. Joe was the Master of the Cheshire Hunt with whom Willie also hunted. My Melody Parkes's sire is the 1983 Derby winner Teenoso. Joe was telling Willie that the filly was very sharp and that I thought a lot of her.

'She will never win a five-furlong-sprint as a two-year-old, being by Teenoso,' says the brash Willie, which led to the bet.

First time out, on 17 April 1995 in the EBF Cap Heaton Maiden Stakes at Newcastle over five furlongs, My Melody Parkes won by three and a half lengths. In fact, the filly was even good enough to run third in the Queen Mary at Royal Ascot.

Joe could never get the account settled until tonight, via me. As the ex-John Peel was staying in Barbados at the time, I was able to give Joe the money the following day. He very kindly returned it to me, to put towards the Injured Jockeys Holiday Fund.

6

Many Thanks, Lads!

When we arrived in Barbados we found that even Stefan, the pro at the Sandy Lane Golf Club, had heard about my retirement. When Michael Jarvis and I went down to the club for a drink, Stefan, like many others, said, 'You're not really retiring, are you? Why?'

The answer is a combination of things. For starters, I am not getting younger and my battered body received more than its fair share of injuries when I was a jump jockey. In fact, with my arthritis, getting around some days I could be mistaken for Quasimodo, the Hunchback of Notre Dame. Hence, the old carcass needs a bit of TLC before it seizes up altogether. Therefore, I intend to wind down a bit, which won't be easy, as work is all I've known throughout my life.

But no one can go on for ever, and there comes a time when the mind and body both tell you to ease up a bit. Besides, the old man of many outfits often hangs on to the head possy for so long the offspring can't get a turn to bring their knowledge or expertise to the fore and there is no room for change because the old man knows it all. The youngsters have to be given a chance, a point I have proved over the years by the amount of winners I have put the kids on.

It just wouldn't do if all the bosses worked until they were ninety. During last season, I was asked on more than one occasion if I had thought about retiring, which got me thinking. In fact, one day, I said to Antonia Deuters, 'Antonia, I have a surprise for you.'

'Don't tell me,' she said, 'you're going to retire!'

There were also rumours flying around Scotland the year before last that I was about to retire. Some people must have thought my sell-by date was coming up and I needed roughing-off. Now Alan knows my position, he has truly got the brakes off. I am very grateful and pleased that Alan wants to take over, as not all sons want to carry on from their fathers. But the opportunity of a lifetime must be grabbed within the lifetime of that opportunity. I like to think that if Alan needs any advice or help, I will be there to give it, though I very much doubt he will wear red shirts!

He's been riding long enough, so he should be all right.

Alan on a pony and, below, with jockey Gary Carter

PHOTOGRAPH: PROSHOT

Training isn't a job for wimps, especially when the horses are running badly. With more and more red tape, rules and regulations, speed-traps, traffic jams and staff problems, it can be a tough old game, especially on a work morning, when we have three or four meetings on and we are flat out to see as many horses as possible work before setting off for the races, and Flash says, 'So-and-so has not turned in today, boss,' cocking-up the work-list.

Both Jo and I started out from humble beginnings, which is nothing to be ashamed of. We are lucky enough to have been fairly successful in our work. It only takes a few minutes at the end of the day to examine one's conscience. If one can put hand on heart and say one hasn't intentionally robbed, cheated, bullied, done anyone a bad turn, rode rough-shod over or been a prat to anyone today, then that's good.

We have paid for our set-up now and don't have the Midland Bank any more as a partner. We also have an insurance plan tucked away for a rainy day. When we eventually pass the yard on to Alan, if we run low on funds, hopefully he will see his way to treating his poor old parents now and again – provided he hasn't blown the lot in the meantime. Not that our Alan goes out of his way to throw money about. He can be a bit like the man who couldn't bear to see another man starve so turned his head the other way,

It is a terrible sadness that our youngest son Sam cannot be part of the action. Sam was so keen on the yard as a little fellow. When he was nine or ten, he would set off every morning for school with Alan while his mum and I, plus the rest of our crew, would be riding out. At least once a week, Sam would catch the string up on a horse that he had tacked up himself, giving me all sorts of excuses about missing the bus and the like. You could not keep Sam out of that yard at any price. Horses were the only thing he thought about.

To keep me out of trouble with the school authorities, I sent Sam to work for Paddy Prendergast Junior, the Irish trainer, a year before he was due to finish school, as kids could leave school in Ireland a year earlier than in Britain. I didn't have time to be watching Sam all the time, as we worked every minute God sent. Looking back on Sam's school reports as a ten-year-old, he was no dud. He had good results. He got ninety-one per cent for mathematics – perhaps with an eye to calculating the odds later on. Alan rode well. He had a few rides as an amateur, but quickly got too heavy. Sam was a natural and a great little rider. I was so proud of him, especially when he rode winners for other yards.

Racing is the only sport where the ambulance follows the athletes around whilst they are working. On 5 March 1985, that awful day at Sedgefield, it had to make a stop and pick up our Sam from a fall off Solares in the novice chase. He was just nineteen and a jockey was the only thing he had ever wanted to be. Sam suffered so badly with head injuries that he has been in and out of hospitals ever since. He now walks with the aid of elbow crutches or gets around in a wheelchair. It's such a shame – but lots of families have a cross to bear.

Sam has always been keen on football and in that department his school report said: 'Martin [Sam] has shown both enthusiasm and skill on the sportsfield and he has been a valuable member of the school football team.' Neil Doughty, his old weighing-room mucker, used too take him quite a bit to see Newcastle play. When I get a bit more time, I will be able to take him myself. But I would rather he supported a proper team, like Leeds United.

At one stage, we hoped Sam might take up a job in the office but, because of his injuries, he finds it hard to concentrate for very long. Anyway, he takes after me too much and loves the outdoors too well too be tied to a desk.

It has been well documented that we built the yard and the gallops from scratch, but it took many more pairs of hands to build the Moss Side Racing set-up than just ours. In those early days, when we first started to work on the property, the locals probably thought of us as some sort of joke as we never stopped grafting, whatever the time or the weather. Lancashire was a non-racing area so maybe they just couldn't appreciate how dedicated horsemen could be.

However, we got going and managed to clock-up a few winners. The village of Cockerham got better known as a result, but instead of sharing our fame with us, certain locals became a bit resentful, hostile even. Had the boot been on the other foot, and a neighbouring farmer had reared cattle that won prizes at county shows, I like to think that I would have taken pride in his success. However, I don't think the locals see us as a source of pride and I cannot remember a time when we could look out of our bedroom window and not see a dirty big muck-heap close to one of our properties.

Over the years we have been fortunate to have some great staff in our squad and without them our rise from near-poverty could not have happened. To show my gratitude, I will mention a few. The first person we employed at our first yard at Arksey near Doncaster was John Spouse, now Clive Brittain's travelling head-lad. Rob Earnshaw (not the Dickinson's jockey) joined us from school at around the same time. They were great kids and I am indebted to them. The three of us virtually demolished the old Moss Side farm and created the foundations for the lovely place you see today. Everything that could be burned, was. We had a fire that never went out for three weeks. The ozone layer has never been the same since.

Chris Searle, a young lass who worked for us at Arksey, came to us straight from school. In fact, she helped at the yard at weekends before she left school. One Sunday, she cycled down to the yard but had to go back home after an hour to change into her Sunday best to compete in the beauty queen pageant in her village of Scawsby. She won the contest then got changed and biked back to the yard for evening stables as if nothing had happened. She used to set her stable boxes beautifully – the days when we bedded down with straw. She used to put a neat twist in front of the doorway – which reminds me of trainer Alan Bailey. One day, when Alan had some owners visiting his yard, he said to one of the lads, 'Make sure you do a nice twist in the doorway when the owners come round, and tell the other lads, too.' The lad in question said to the rest of the staff, 'The old man must be going round the effing bend. He said when the owners come round, we all have to dance in the doorways!'

Chris is a smashing girl and was a great asset at Moss Side, turning horses out second to none for years. Later she married a local farmer, Josh Rossall, and they have two lovely kids, a boy and a girl. Chris now has a livery yard at their farm and takes in our sick, sorry, lame or lazy horses for rest, change or whatever.

In later years, 'Cock of the North' jockey Kevin Darley did his bit getting our yard going, as did our second head-man Kevin Ryan, now himself a successful trainer based at Hambleton.

It just would be a crime for me not to mention John Carroll, as loyal and hard a worker as you could ever meet. John rode more than five hundred winners for our yard. There is no need to say too much regarding them – he was getting paid. But I would need to take out a mortgage to repay him for the fun we had. JC could drive anything that moved, do any job and was strong and fearless. Only rarely did we not see eye to eye. When John left the yard, we lost much more than the stable jockey and employee of twelve years. We were a good team and lots of marriages don't last as long as we did. He and I must have travelled a million miles to hundreds of race-meetings together. At times, I have been near to crying with laughter at his antics. He was so unpredictable. Honestly, at times you didn't know what he was going to do next. One day we were having stalls practice when the horse ridden by our apprentice Willie Hollick dived under the starting stalls, dragging off poor Willie and breaking his leg. As you can imagine, we were all as sullen and sick as butchers' dogs – gutted we were. When the ambulance arrived, its driver and his mate left it in our indoor school and hurried down to the stalls with a stretcher to recover the stricken rider. After JC had done his horse up, he climbed into the ambulance, changed his crash helmet for the peaked hat the driver had left in the cab, put the flashing lights on and drove a couple of circuits round our school. He then backed the ambulance up to the bottom entrance of the school and gave the crew a hand in with Willie, who was in screaming agony until he saw yer man with the hat on. He almost fell off the stretcher with laughing.

I had better not say too much about John's driving or plod may pay him a visit and take him away. But once, and not for a change, we were in a rush on our way to Chester races. Meeting a long tailback on the M6, JC pulled straight on to the hard shoulder. Jockey Jimmy Quinn followed us, as John was going to show him a short-cut through Chester. We were passing cars, vans, wagons and buses wholesale. Some of the drivers were shouting abuse, blowing horns, flashing their lights and making rude gestures. After three or four miles, we came up behind a Black Maria. The bobbies must have seen our car in the emergency lane in their mirror as none of the other drivers would let us merge back on to the motorway. The boys in blue beckoned John out of the car and gave him a real bollocking. Jimmy can barely see over the steering-wheel, he is so small. Looking like a joy-rider, he was sitting in his car absolutely crapping himself. The punters in the Black Martia must have been able to hear the police getting at John and were going mad, kicking the van's back doors, and yelling, 'Tell them to eff off, pal.' Although they were furious, the law men let us go, their hands being full enough with the prisoners, but I am sure they would love to have added John to their load.

Wally Hagger, who originated from London and worked for our yard for about ten years, was regarded as part of the family. A good lad, he was always confident in his work and could do most jobs. Unfortunately, he wasn't one of the best riders we have had through our hands, although O.I.Oyston took him round a couple of times to pass the post first in races. Wally left our yard following a bust-up with one of the other lads.

A few years ago, as we were getting more horses and we needed extra room, Jo, Alan and I decided that we would knock down the existing stables on the far side of the school, along with the hay-shed at the rear of them, and extend more new boxes into the paddock. The A-Team set to, its mainstays being Alan, John Carroll and Wally. We demolished and cremated the old wooded stables, built up the whole area with tons and tons of hard-core, put in drains and the foundations for nineteen new boxes, which we bought from Hodgesons of Barnard Castle who erected them in just four days. John Curwen, a local contractor, tracked in the foundations and laid the tarmac in the new yard. In two weeks, we had the boxes painted up with horses in. Wimpey's would have been proud of us.

Casualty Call, the first runner from our Cockerham base, won at Worcester on the 2 September 1972, ridden by Pat Buckley and owned by David Hall, who has a two-year-old with us now, some twenty-seven years later.

PHOTOGRAPH: JOHN GRANT

Casualty Call winning at Worcester on the 2 September 1972,
ridden by Pat Buckley and owned by David Hall

We have a good head-man in Tony McWilliams (Flash) and as good a secretary as you would find anywhere in his missus, Helen. Both have worked for us for years.

There are many more good people who have done their bit to make the yard what it is today. Too many too mention, but I sincerely thank them all.

7

Success at Last

Alan picked up his mother and me from Manchester Airport on Monday, 18 January 1999. Usually the yard has a winner or two when we are on holiday. Unfortunately, this year it had drawn a blank. The weather had been atrocious at home in our absence, as I found when walking on our middle grass gallop on our return. It was like a big sponge, holding all the unwelcome rain that had been dropped on it. The horses looked well and my three and a half couple of dogs went bananas when they saw their old pal back.

Roger the vicar rang to ask me if he could bring the Bishop of Blackburn down the following afternoon to have a look round our estate. What a friendly and thoroughly interesting person he turned out to be. 'Call me Stephen!' he said, when Roger introduced him to me. He wanted to know all about the horses and racing. He's the first important person to visit our yard that I haven't tried to sell a horse to; especially slow of me as we still have a few two-year-olds for sale. Must be losing my grip! Perhaps I could do with a few lessons from one of our owners, Ken Oliver, who, with Willie Stephenson, restarted Doncaster Sales in 1962. Ken even sold a horse to Sir Winston Churchill.

I hope Helen's wedding proved a bit more successful than the horse Helen's Wedding we ran the other day at Southwell. Although she goes quite well at home, she got so far behind at the races, you would have needed a good pair of binoculars to sight her. Paul Gascoigne, 'Gazza', could cry faster than she gallops. When you buy the horses as yearlings, you don't always get what you want. You get what you get, and she is very moderate. I am afraid I will have to find another address for her. She cannot stay here dragging on the rations. The 'To Let' board won't need to go on the door as thankfully we have a couple of horses waiting for a space in the yard at the moment.

Life is rewarding when one gets letters like these:

From : Milo Corbett

C/o Equine Nutritional Consultancy Ltd
Westfield Farm
Lambourn Road
East Garston
Near Hungerford
Berkshire
RG17 7HD

26th January 1999

Dear Mr and Mrs Berry, (and horses and dogs)

You probably won't remember me, but I was one of the boys who walked from Murrayfield to Cardiff and Twickenham a couple of summers ago to raise money for Spinal Research Charities. You were very kind and let us camp overnight in one of your paddocks and went far beyond the call of duty in providing a fantastic barbecue and lots of beer for us!

I saw in the Racing Post at the end of last year that this coming season will be your last in charge at Moss Side before your son takes over the licence. I am just writing to wish you another very successful year and to wish you all the luck in the world in your quest for that group one winner. Though I know you'll still be very much involved in the running of the yard, when the time comes we all wish you both a long and happy "semi-retirement".

With all the hard work you have put into riding and training, your record of success speaks for itself. On behalf of people like us, however, who have benefited so much from all the good works you do behind the public eye for worthy causes, may I wish you both every future success and happiness – both are certainly much deserved.

Please excuse this being a "computered" letter but my handwriting is dreadful!

Yours sincerely
Milo Corbett

Mr & Mrs Jack Berry
Moss Side Racing Stables
Cockerham
Lancaster

P.S. And best wishes from my father, too – as you call him – "the bloodstock agent who smokes for Britain!"

MR J CALDWELL
42 MICKLEHURST RD
MOSSLEY
LANCS
OL5 9NL

DEAR JACK,

I'VE JUST ARRIVED BACK FROM HOLIDAY IN SPAIN. I BORROWED YOUR BOOK LIFE TOUGHER AT THE BOTTOM, FROM MY MATE WHO GOT IT FOR CHRISTMAS. I PICKED THE BOOK UP AT 9·30 AM AND I JUST COULD NOT PUT IT DOWN. I SAT THERE UNTIL I FINISHED IT. I'VE READ QUITE A LOT OF RACING BOOKS BUT I THINK THIS WAS THE BEST I'VE READ. I'M A FLAT RACING FAN BUT I DO HAVE A BET ON THE JUMPS. READING YOUR BOOK HAS CHANGED MY ATTITUDE ON JUMPING. WHEN MY

HORSE WAS IN 2ND OR 3rd I'VE BEEN KNOW TO SHOUT AT THE TELEVISION, FALL YOU B___ TO THE FRONT HORSE. I DON'T THINK I'll be doing THIS ANY MORE NOW I KNOW HOW SERIOUSLY THE JOCKEY CAN GET INJURED. I KNEW THEY GOT BROKEN BONES ECT BUT I DID NOT KNOW PEOPLE GOT KILLED. SORRY FOR BEING SO NAIVE. GIVE MY BEST TO YOUR SAM AND THANKS AGAIN FOR THE PLEASURE YOU GIVE ME IN READING YOUR BOOK.

YOURS
SINCERLEY
John Caldwell

Unfortunately, my penfriend in London takes a different view. He (unless of course it's a woman, in which case 'slapper' would be too nice a word for the bag) wrote to me a few times, this particular one being the first. The naughty words in the others make them X-certificate. My missus has been known to say that I sleep with one eye open. Is it any wonder!?

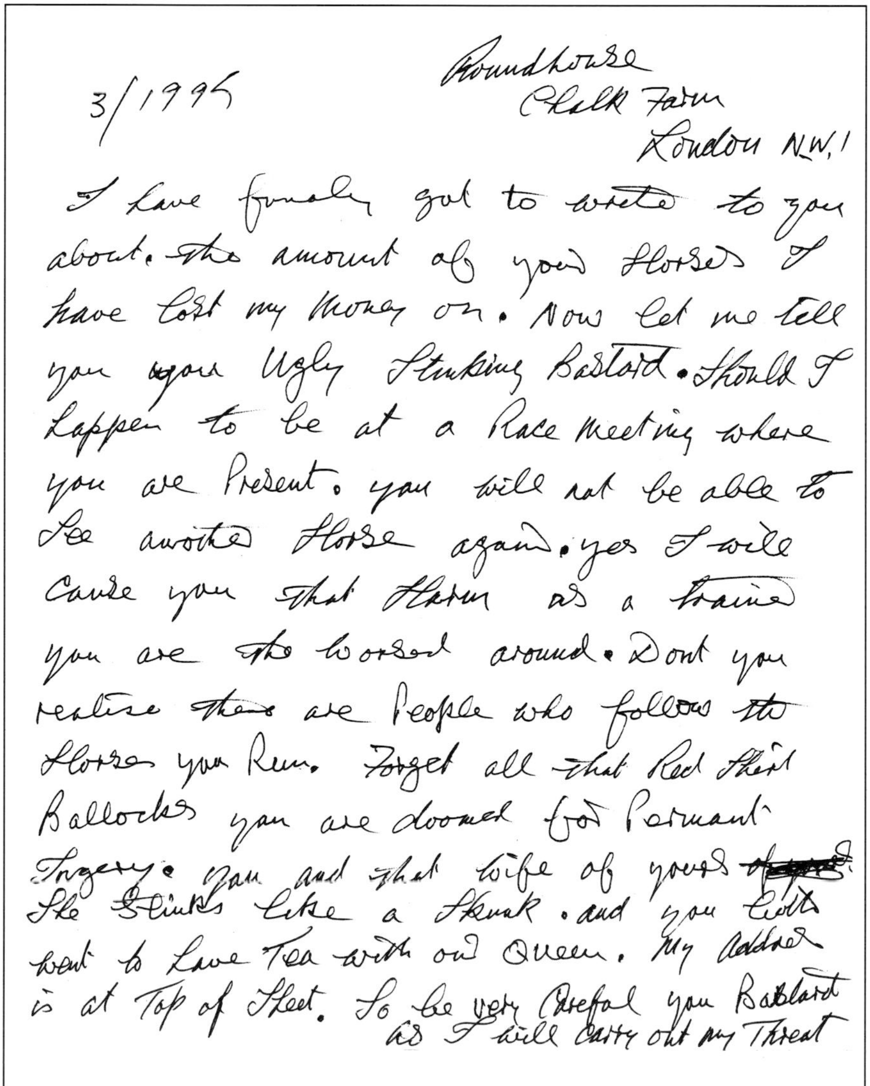

3/1995

Roundhouse
Chalk Farm
London N.W.1

I have finally got to write to you about the amount of your Horses I have lost my money on. Now let me tell you you are Ugly Stinking Bastard. Should I happen to be at a Race meeting where you are Present, you will not be able to See another Horse again, yes I will Cause you that Harm as a Trainer you are the Worsed around. Don't you realise there are People who follow the Horses you Run. Forget all that Red Shirt Ballocks you are doomed for Permant Surgery. you and that Wife of yours She Stinks like a Skunk. and you Both went to have Tea with our Queen. My Address is at Top of Sheet. So be very Careful you Bastard as I will Carry out my Threat

Call it a wicked sense of humour if you like, but I could not help smiling at the headline in the *Racing Post* the other day: 'Straps move closer'. It meant we are going to have to declare tongue-straps in races at the overnight stage. Yet more information rammed down punters' necks in betting-shops! Sir Tom Finney and I opened a betting-shop in Preston recently but we were only in the shop an hour or so; what with all the activity going on, with continual interruptions during the races and different announcements on the many screens, interviews with trainers, jockeys, even stable-staff, I came out with a splitting headache.

Punters get so much information: the findings of stewards' inquiries, declaration of jockeys and gadgets, trainers' explanations, advice in the papers, timings, statistics, SIS, phone tipping lines and the like. I have even heard silly calls from people who would like to have horses' weights published, like greyhounds'. The next thing they will want to know is if the horse did a whoopsie before it left home!

A far cry from the days when the starters of big fields called to the jockeys: 'Bad horses and non-tryers at the back, please.' I honestly wonder if all this available knowledge enables anyone to back more winners than they used to. Gone are the days of old-fashioned gambles, when the cunning horsemen would not have told their own mothers the time of day. Some trainers have even been known to kip by themselves on the lead up to a coup just in case they talked in their sleep and their partners heard them mention a horse's name. Picture the scene. The Derek Thomson of the day ringing the trainer's wife whilst the old man is working his horses, 'Have you heard or has he said anything yet?' If there is the slightest smell of a plot nowadays, it isn't long before everyone knows.

Following a few near misses, with photographs going the wrong way for our yard, it took us to Wednesday, 27 January at Wolverhampton to claim our first winner of the season. Mary Jane, this time ridden by Iona Wands, another of our apprentices, was the victor – a welcome change of luck for Iona, Mary Jane being her first ride back since she broke a finger six weeks ago. Iona (seven stone) walks out with Paul Fessey (seven stone ten pounds). Both are good little riders. If they have some

Owner John Forsyth, agent Jimmy Byrne and stud owner Terry Holdcroft
look as if they are organising a coup

kids during my semi-retirement, I wouldn't mind being their agent. If that pair can't breed jockeys, then who can?

Thankfully, we did not have to wait long for our next winner, as nine-year-old Palacegate Touch (Archie) won at Lingfield the following day, ridden by Paul Bradley, another one of the stars from our apprentice academy. It was Archie's twenty-sixth win from one hundred and six runs.

Red Venus kept the roll going by winning a small race at Southwell the day after. As the late and legendary jump trainer Arthur Stephenson used to say, 'Little fish are sweet,' and in racing they maintain you should keep yourself in the best company and your horses in the worst. I'm saying nothing about the company but one couldn't go much lower to win a race than Red Venus did at 3.55 p.m. in the Foley Selling Stakes on 29 January on the all-weather at Southwell. That's where Red Venus won for the first time in her career from twelve attempts, picking up £1,872.40 in prize-money. As it happened, this little fish didn't taste too sweet, as we were bid up to seven thousand pounds to buy her back at the auction, which left us seriously out of pocket for the privilege of winning a race. I am not really screaming, as it was the filly's first run over seven furlongs and she won so easily. She looks an improving sort that could go on and win again at this trip or even further.

Exactly one week after Mary Jane's win at Wolverhampton, she went back to the same course for a stab at the claimer with a price-tag of six thousand pounds. On this occasion, she was ridden by yet another of our budding Lester Piggotts, Paul Roberts; I try to share out the rides amongst the kids on these moderate horses this time of year.

The filly started 11–4 favourite and finished third. Newmarket trainer Robert Cowell claimed her on behalf of Paradise Racing. He can't have been at Doncaster Sales when Mary Jane was sold for just sixteen hundred guineas. As Del-Boy would say, 'A nice little earner.'

Alan was in charge at Wolverhampton as I was away conducting the auction at Ken Oliver's eighty-fifth-birthday bash at Kelso racecourse, which was arranged by Fran Marshall, Scottish racing's public-relations officer. All the proceeds of the evening, which had attracted around seventy very (as you can see by the prices they paid for the items auctioned) generous people, went to the Injured Jockeys Holiday Fund. Jonjo O'Neill recovered a bit of the two hundred and sixty pounds he paid for the art figurines, as in the bar at the Roxburgh Hotel, where we stayed the night, the tight little git asked me if I would like a drink. When settling my account the following morning, I noticed bar drinks (£25.70) had been charged to my account!

It was an absolutely brilliant night. Bill Harvey, John Morgan and Jim McGrath were the speakers and very good they were, too. With all the events and spin-offs, the holiday fund will benefit considerably.

The first Sunday in February was the day we launched this year's

Peter Beaumont, Tom Kemp and JB at the auction in aid of the Injured Jockeys Holiday Fund

'Red-Shirt Brigade' club. Around forty members turned out to see their horses work in pairs on our fifteen-foot-wide all-weather wood-chip gallop and hack back in a nice tight bunch. I would love to have done the work on grass but weather conditions made that impossible.

It makes me wonder how on earth trainers managed to train and get horses fit before we had all-weather gallops. Jonjo O'Neill was telling me that Aidan O'Brien sometimes took his horses to work on an uphill all-weather gallop at his old yard at Pilltown, half an hour's ride away in a horse-box. John Magnier grumbled that it was ridiculous with the facilities they had at Ballydoyle. To stop any aggravation, Aidan had a six-furlong, uphill, all-weather, thirty-feet-wide gallop built. When Charlie Swan asked Alan Roche, Jonjo's head-lad, why Aidan made the gallop so wide, Alan replied, 'So Mick Maloney [the ex-jump jockey who used to ride for us] could ride upsides!'

Amongst the members of the Red-Shirt Brigade present was Alex Ferguson, fresh from his triumphant win the day before when his team

JB with Jonjo O'Neill

had beaten Nottingham Forest 8–1. We all had a buffet lunch in our indoor school, followed by drinks in the house.

The Red-Shirt Brigade is managed by Pete and Sandy Murphy. The members make a one-off payment of three thousand pounds for a share in the club's six horses; there is a maximum of fifty shareholders. At the end of the Flat season all the horses are sold as they stand at public auction without reserve, whether they be good, bad or indifferent. The idea is to give the members a bit of fun which, whatever happens, cannot cost more than three thousand pounds. Last year the club had thirty-six runners all over the country and among them were six winners, five seconds and three thirds.

We have some magic Sunday afternoons in the house at the yard when I put aside time to see owners and chat about their horses. We have tea, coffee or maybe something a little stronger. On Sunday, 14 February, we had a great bit of crack as J. K. Brown, known as 'The Captain', came. John (no relation to Captain Brown, the ex-starter) is called The Captain because he has had horses with us for twenty-one years. He arrived with his partner in horses, John Shaw, and they, along with Roy and Norma Peebles, the proud owners of old Amron (Ronnie), were in great form, reminiscing about horses past and present that we have had in our care.

Roy's long-time friend, Murray Grubb, who owns Persian Fayre, has a dodgy ticker and has been fitted with a heart valve. Murray loves his racing, but it isn't any good for him to get too excited. When Persian Fayre, stable name The Rug, won at York, ridden by Kieren Fallon, Murray (well, even Sheikh Hamdan would get excited winning a race at York) went deathly white and said to Roy, 'I don't think I can make it to the winning enclosure to greet my horse.' Roy, without batting an eyelid, was quick to ask, 'Which bookie did you back the horse with?' It seemed the bookie, knowing Murray, had not given him a ticket. 'What's his name then,' Roy pressed him more urgently.

It is very hard for apprentices to carry on riding winners when they have ceased to claim an allowance. As Paul Fessey lost his claim today – Tuesday, 16 February – Granada TV came to our yard and followed Paul around for most of the morning, like a dog would a bitch on heat, filming a documentary on the lifestyle of a young jockey.

In the evening, Jo and I met up with Alex and Kath Ferguson for a meal at the Lincoln Restaurant in Manchester. Prior to that, we had all attended the grand opening of the Quality Hotel in Manchester, where Alex did the honours. None other than spiky-haired Gary Rhodes is chef at the hotel.

On Wednesday night, Jo and I went to see Manchester United play Arsenal, a match which resulted in a 1–1 draw. I bet there were some choice words in the dressing-room from Mr Ferguson when Dwight Yorke missed that penalty.

8

If Ever I Felt Like Crying . . .

Although we had a runner, rather than spend my Saturday night at Wolverhampton sand meeting on 20 February, I met up with Country and Western singer Bob Kendall at Kirkby Stephen's Working Men's Club to earn a few bob for the Injured Jockeys Holiday Fund. That morning I had received a letter from 'Gentleman Joe' Mercer OBE to say he is holding his golf charity day at Sandford Springs Golf Club on 26 April, this year in aid of the IJHF and the Wessex Children's Hospice. I hope everyone has a super day. Well done, Joe.

On Monday, 22 February, Carlisle's jump fixture was the G. W. Richards Memorial Day, when all the races were named after the late trainer's famous horses. When we finished work, Jo, Flash and I went to Carlisle, where it was bitterly cold with near gale-force winds. But for all that, we had a very enjoyable day. Flash worked for GWR a few years ago, so it was nice for him to see some of his old mates and have a bit of a gas with them. The cold must have been showing on me, as racecourse director James Westall kindly asked me into the directors' private room for a drink. After a Cumbrian-sized whisky, I felt a good bit warmer.

Carlisle was Gordon's local course for the last thirty years of the National Hunt legend's career, during which he trained over two thousand winners, including two Grand Nationals and a five-timer at Carlisle. Not only was GWR good with his horses, both Ron Barry and Jonjo O'Neill were champion jockeys when they rode for him. Gordon wasn't bad at preparing trainers, either, of which the likes of Jonjo, Dick Allen, Martin Todhunter, Colin Parker, Malcolm Jefferson and now Gordon's son Nicky are indisputable proof.

Wednesday, 24 February, a lovely spring day, was the first time we let our most forward two-year-olds stride on, even though lots of people think that we gallop the guts off the youngsters around Christmas. One youngster, Nifty Major, looked very sharp but we will need to go carefully with him as he gets very busy and comes from a family well known for being highly strung. I don't want to blow his mind by asking him any serious questions too early.

After watching our novice chaser Carlisle Banditos finish second to Manasis, beaten just half a length in a field of sixteen at Doncaster where he jumped like a buck, I dashed off to watch Palacegate Jack on the Racing Channel in the owners' and trainers' tea-shed. Winging round the corner, I lost my footing and came a real purler. Had the racecourse doctor seen it, he would probably have stood me down for a couple of days. Picking myself up and feeling a right divvy, I was just in time to catch the last two furlongs, where Jack finished fourth, beaten heads and necks, not doing a tap. Jack has a lot of ability but isn't too keen on sharing it with the punters, preferring to keep most of it to himself. Later on an observant racegoer asked me for my autograph and said, 'You need a lot more schooling or you should take more water with it!'

On our way back from Doncaster, we passed our Wolverhampton box. I had a look across to see if Jack was driving, as there's not much he can't do. Jack is as cunning as a box of monkeys and probably knows more about the game than Jim McGrath of Timeform. Jack was Lester Piggott's last British winner – at Haydock Park on the 5 October 1994.

February 25 and it's The Bride's birthday. Tonight, I am taking her and a few of our staff to Bumbles, a nice little restaurant in our village. My reasoning is if she gets popped-up, she doesn't have far to travel. The missus must be quite popular as she received fourteen cards and six bunches of flowers.

When she was fifty, as a special treat to celebrate the occasion, I booked a white chauffeur-driven Roller to take us to Ryecroft Hall, an up-market restaurant on the way to Blackpool. When Jo came out of the house and saw the Rolls-Royce with the dolled-up driver courteously holding the door open for her, she said, 'It's a bit OTT, isn't it? There was no need for that.' I very nearly had to call our stall-handlers with a hood to load her up. So I'm playing it low-key this year. Lucky for her that our local fish-and-chip shop is closed on Thursdays.

The next day was not a day to be celebrating. After the second lot, I needed to make my way over to Bilton-in-Ainsty in Yorkshire for the funeral of sixty-nine-year-old Anne Charlton, daughter of ex-trainer Sam Hall, sister of trainer Sally Hall and niece of my old boss, Charlie Hall. Anne's other sister Jean married Newmarket trainer Ryan Jarvis, whose son Willie is now the master of Phantom House yard. Her cousin, Maurice Camacho, trained in Malton for many years before handing over to his daughter, Julie. The whole family is steeped in racing history. I grew up with Anne and Sally at Charlie Hall's now defunct yard in the village of Towton, as the sisters went to live with their Uncle Charlie following their father's early death.

The church was packed and the service was relayed outside to the punters who couldn't get an inside stall. We sang 'Praise My Soul the King of Heaven' and 'Love Divine All Loves Excelling', but the last hymn summed her up perfectly for me – 'All Things Bright and Beautiful'. When we were in church I could visualise the guv'nor, Charlie Hall (whom Anne thought the world of), walking to meet her with his arms outstretched, and Anne running towards him, both looking so happy.

That night, I met up with most of our staff at Quattro's Italian Restaurant on the A6 near Garstang, to attend a joint party for four of our most loyal workers who are leaving us. I tell you, if ever I felt like crying, it was tonight.

Paul Roberts, one of our star apprentices, who has now served his time, is a lovely horseman who has worked for us since leaving school. Paul is going to ride as first jockey to the Belgium trainer, Claude Dondy, who stables sixty horses.

Mette Hanssen, a good little rider, has spent two years with us, having come to gain some experience. She's a great kid and has got herself a nice number riding for a yard with twenty horses back home in Norway.

Beverley Kendall, our amateur, is going to work for Middleham trainer Ann Swinbank, hoping to get more chances to ride in the jump races which she loves. Bev rides well, has a nice disposition and a good attitude. She is courting one of our travelling head-lads, Graham Scope, an excellent work-rider who is also bound for Ann Swinbank as head-lad.

What a hole that has left in the yard. If I said I am gutted I would be putting it mildly. The only consolation is all four of them have genuinely left for promotion in pursuit of their careers. Hand on heart, I honestly want them to get on and really do well, as they all deserve to. But my feelings at the moment are of sorrow and loneliness. Staff the calibre of those four are hard to come by, but life goes on.

A sportsmen's dinner and talk-in was held following racing at Musselburgh racecourse on the last Saturday in February. Although you may think I couldn't sell life-belts to terminally ill millionaires on a sinking ship, I was asked to conduct the auction. A set of Robert Sangster's colours, carried by Distinctly North when he won the 1990 Group 2 Flying Childers Stakes, made £500; a signed Manchester United shirt, donated by Alex Ferguson, fetched £375; and a signed photographic print by Claire Williams of all the Newmarket trainers of 1966 also realised £375. A nice little earner for the cause.

As the reveleries went on until very late, I decided to stay over at the Woodside Hotel, which is opposite the two-furlong pole. The next day was the first Sunday for a long time that I didn't need to visit Gladys to chop her sticks and get her coal in for her fire as on Friday the poor old dear fell down and ended up in hospital.

As I was in Scotland, I travelled back on the A7 route to enable me to visit Ken Oliver, who hasn't been in good health recently. It was the day Ken's local hunt, the Berwickshire, were holding their point-to-point. I borrowed a flat-cap and a pair of rubber boots from Ken and went along. Although it was freezing cold and pouring with rain, it was nice to see and chat to a lot of people from the jumping world I don't get to see very often.

While driving back through Hawick on my way home, I saw in my rear mirror a police car following me. After seven or eight miles it passed me, and, as expected, the driver put his flashing lights on for me to stop, which I did. 'Have you an exemption certificate for not wearing your seat-belt sir?' asked the lawman. 'Yes,' I said. 'As I have received a few clavicle fractures over the years, I carry a certificate from my doctor,' and handed over the evidence. 'Sorry to have troubled you, sir,' he said, and off he went. Had I been breathalysed the placing would have remained unaltered, as I had only drunk two glasses of red wine with the meal at the bash the evening before and at the point-to-point I had just had a can of lager with the Jockey Club starter, John Leach. I didn't tell John what I had written about him earlier or I would probably have had to buy my own!

Today is 10 March and the first day we haven't had rain since 9 February, and that's official. Marie Matthews, who owns the two-year-old Gem of Wisdom, came this morning to watch him work, along with her husband Barry, her son John and Northern steward John Day. Later on, we all went to Bumbles for lunch. Barry is a keen vegetable grower and was telling me about his produce winning at various shows; listening to him reminded me of Dick Earnshaw, a neighbour of ours, when we trained at Arksey. As we were riding out past Dick's place, he would call to me, 'Look at the size of those pears, Jack,' pointing up a tree. On the way back he would meet us at this gate. 'Did you ever see a better cabbage than that? Feel how firm it is.' Or, 'My peas are as big as marbles this year.' The lads would be cracking up and I would have to keep a straight face. On a weekend, he would sell a bit of his produce to the locals. One day, a mother sent her offspring down to his pad. 'My mum would like two pounds of potatoes and a pound of beetroot, please, Mr Earnshaw.' 'There's your potatoes, came the reply, 'Now go back and tell your mum I don't cut my beetroot in half for anybody!'

It's 8.45 p.m. and I'm watching the replay of the Manchester United versus Chelsea match when Alan comes steaming in from the yard. Seeing the match on TV, he says, 'The boss [A. Ferguson] of that lot's two-year-old [Ninety Degrees] is cast in his box, thrashing about. I need help getting him up.' Thankfully the horse was all right. And what a good result for Manchester United, with their 2–0 win.

Tomorrow, we are taking twelve of our two-year-olds for a stalls trial and gallop at Wolverhampton. John Carroll, Gary Carter and Kevin Darley (the main jockeys we use) will be taking part, together with our Paul Fessey, Iona Wands and Paul Bradley. I'm not bragging but complaining when I put my hand on my heart and say that, except for hacking around the paddocks when they were getting broken, it will be the first time their little feet have touched grass, it has been so wet.

It will also be the first time we have clipped-out our youngsters fully. Horses nowadays are so well-handled when very young, they don't seem to mind being clipped. Trying to keep the poor little beggars from getting sweaty is near impossible when they carry long woolly coats. The only alternative would be to ride them in the indoor school every day, only that would bore the pants off them.

Talking of clipping reminds me of my days as a freelance jockey, recently married. To say I was struggling at the time would be an understatement. In those days we had harsher winters. It would freeze and snow for days on end, losing us lots of jump meetings and me rides. To make ends meet, I ran an advert in our local paper: *Horses and ponies clipped. Ring Arksey 54126.*

One day I was called-out to clip a big grey belonging to Bill Ibbertson, a permit trainer whose horse was stabled in the yard of a pub called the Drum in Thurnscoe, near Rotherham. As soon as I switched on the electric clippers, the brute went ballistic. In unison, the two people there said, 'It always does that, that's why it's never been clipped.' Thankfully, one of the men, Jeff Fletcher, who worked for Bill (and later became a trainer in Newmarket), said, 'The big ignorant bugger's never had a proper man like me to hold it though.' I loved the sound of that, as I had travelled fifteen miles or so in my car to do the job and I couldn't afford to lose out on my four-pound clipping charge. We put a twitch on the horse's nose and stuffed his ears with cotton-wool, but he still messed about quite a lot. This fellow Jeff had got it right. The horse was a big ignorant bugger and the quicker I could get its wool off the better it would be for all of us, as he was a real handful and wasn't sticking to Queensberry Rules. With a struggle, I managed to clip both sides. The horse had been on the floor a couple of times and so had Jeff. At one stage the beggar had both his front legs on Jeff's shoulders. When I tried to clip his head, the BIB really went bananas. I don't know how Jeff came to be behind him, as he still had hold of the twitch, but he gave Jeff a nasty kick in his privates and my man flaked out on me.

Sundown was the horse's actual name although I never heard Jeff or the other guy call him by it. At a later date, I rode him work. When Jeff called him BIB he missed the U for useless in between the I and the Bs. No horse can help being slow, but this boat abused the definition. It was truly pathetic. Anyway, I gave him a couple of smacks more than I usually would have done, but still Sundown could not have won the gallop if he had set off ten minutes before the others. Hitting a horse when out of contention would nowadays cost a jockey a few days' suspension, but Sunnyboy was lucky it was me riding him, not Jeff Fletcher.

Back to Wolverhampton. The youngsters went really well, although the sand surface was probably not ideal. But it was a welcome change from their usual routine and very educational. I'm sure it did the juveniles a power of good and with their new haircuts they looked great.

We shouldn't grumble too much about the weather we've had as there have been people a lot worse off than us. Today Trainer James Hetherton was on page 3 – not in the *Sun*, giving us a flash, but in the *Racing Post* – towing a boat and wading waist high in water, rescuing an old lady from her flooded home at Norton near Malton in Yorkshire. James's father told me that James went to rescue an uncommonly good-looking young lady who said, 'No, thanks, I would rather drown than risk going with you in that boat.'

On 1 April 1999, stable staff are set for a pay rise. We have always paid our lads and lasses more than the minimum wage. Stable employees are not the best paid employees in the country but they are far better off than they used to be. As an apprentice, I earned five shillings (twenty-five pence) a week, with my food and clothes thrown in. If you could have seen the Tadcaster Co-Op drainpipe trousers that Anne bought for us kids – they were something else. I bet outsiders thought we were going to a fancy-dress party or came from a young offenders' home. No wonder I tried so hard to save and buy my own.

In today's reckoning, five shillings would be worth around ten pounds. So we weren't exactly overpaid. Ten Woodbine cigarettes cost around one shilling and fourpence, a pint of beer about the same. The picture house in Tadcaster charged two and six (twelve and a half

PHOTOGRAPH: RACING POST (ROSS PARRY)

James Heatherton's picture in the Racing Post

pence). If we went to the pictures on Friday, pay day, bought a pint and a packet of fags – that was it! Stony-broke for the rest of the week.

In view of the pay-rise and the never-ending fuel increases to run the wagons, the extras will unfortunately have to be passed on to the owners, a thing I hate doing, though I'm sure it is better for me to bring the fees into line now rather than leave it for Alan to do in his first year in office.

I have never found it easy to ask for a rise. As a jockey I was a council member for the North. We held a meeting at the Bridge Inn at Boroughbridge. In those days National Hunt jockeys were getting ten guineas a ride. Attending the meeting were Larry Major, Paddy Farrell, Johnny East, Jack Boddy, Gerry Scott, Nimrod Wilkinson, Stan Hayhurst and myself. The main topic was whether we should try for an increase of two guineas in riding fees. When we put it to the vote, I was the only jockey who said, 'Leave it as it is. The owners can't afford to pay any more. We are biting the hand that feeds us.'

I have checked the figures out with my old pal, Paddy Farrell, who tragically broke his back in the 1964 Grand National on Border Flight and has been in a wheelchair ever since (thirty-five years at the time of writing, nearly half his life). Today the jump boys get eighty-seven pounds per ride, and they earn it too, but following my showing at the Boroughbridge meeting, you could say it's no thanks to me.

It's 10.00 a.m. on Wednesday, 17 March and the lads have just gone for their breakfast after riding two lots out. We have a number of horses on the walkers with tack on, so the riders will take them off and work them on their return. It's a lovely day. The birds are singing, the two-year-olds are on the gallops and playing the right tunes.

Next week, we make entries for the opening meeting at Doncaster. For the first time Windsor is scheduled for the same day. At this stage, I have entered Charlie Sparrowhawk's Paris Star in the Brocklesby. Originally I intended sending Paris Star to Windsor as Charlie, who isn't blessed with the best of health, lives near Windsor. I explained this to Kevin Darley after he had ridden a good piece of work on Paris Star, and Kevin said, 'Doesn't he know how bad the traffic gets around Windsor?' 'You're not listening, Kevin. The owner lives there.' 'Well, hasn't he got a telly or the

Racing Channel that he could catch it on. Or, if he went to Windsor, he could see the horse run on SIS.' These jockeys are so thoughtful.

Andy Miller's Red Sun had been entered for the Windsor maiden, but the race had to be abandoned because heavy rain had made the course unsafe. Bob Tanner's Singsong was entered for the Grey Friars and our own Melodic Heights for the seller.

The seller at Doncaster last year proved to be a warm little contest, with Mick Channon's Inya Lake beating our Angus the Bold. Inya Lake went on to win three more races, including the Group 3 Molecomb Stakes at Goodwood, worth £23,725 to the winner. After the race, Inya Lake was bought in for eight thousand two hundred pounds. Les Eyre's owners Diamond Racing claimed Angus the Bold for six thousand pounds. Angus never ran again. I bet the Hambleton Maestro and his cronies were a bit sick buying our man and missing out on the winner. Maybe it will be third time lucky for the Eyre outfit if they buy Melodic Heights at Doncaster, as they also claimed Five-O-Fifty from our yard when she was second at Nottingham, which also did no good.

As soon as we have finished working the horses, Jo and I are travelling to Hereford to stay the night with the Deuters, then it's on to Cheltenham for tomorrow's Gold Cup Day. I love the buzz of that place and I must admit I am keyed up just like a little kid. There is no other race meeting like Cheltenham in the whole world and you can feel the vibes as soon as you reach the car park.

In 1956, I looked after Doorknocker, who won the Champion Hurdle for his owner Clifford Nicholson, trainer Charlie Hall and the crack hurdle jockey of the day, Harry Sprague. Cliff Nick, as we called him behind his back ('sir' to his face, after every sentence), always wore a big red carnation in his lapel, which his chauffeur fetched for him daily. His colours were scarlet and grey and his horses always ran with a white breastplate. After the race, Mr Nicholson took his horse off me to lead him into the winner's enclosure. There were hundreds of people crowded round the horse and, being quite small, I got shuffled to the back. So there was Cliff Nick, immaculately dressed, complete with bowler and monocle, holding on to Doorknocker, looking all over the place, shouting, 'Where's the boy, where's the boy?'

Cliff Nick had quite a few good horses at our yard and I remember that we were all frightened to death of him. In those days stable staff got five pounds for every winner they looked after, although Mr Nicholson only gave us three pounds. But he had such good horses, we could be sure of doing winners and getting to the better meetings. In those days competition in the yards was fierce and it was a great honour to do a good horse. If one of the lads rode your horse out and hadn't groomed and done him up properly, there would just about be a fight over it. Everyone took a real pride in their horses.

Last year was the first Cheltenham I have missed for as long as I can remember. It was because Jo had broken her leg, not from kicking the dogs but through falling off a horse. When it happened, I said, 'What a time to get hurt, just before Cheltenham.'

It is always nice to see some old mates, such as David Mould, Ron Atkins, Ken Bridgewater and many more, to reminisce with. I gave Jenny Pitman, 'The Cuddly One', as John McCririck calls her, a nice big hug as she had just announced her intention to retire at the end of the jump season and hand over to her son Mark.

Our gang, Chris and Antonia, Frazer and Liz Hines, Ian and Marie Goldsmith, did forecasts, tricasts, placepots, jackpots and a private sweep in the big race. I never got a draw, but it was great fun. Palacegate Touch (Archie) won at Lingfield. Jo and I had a shout for him as we watched his race on SIS from the Tote credit shop.

Archie was a bit stiff after we worked him the other day, so we got Bob Kendall, our back man, to sort him out. Bob told us that the horse had a trapped nerve on top of his quarters. Bob's other job is being a Country and Western singer, and a very good one at that. He and I made the tape *Off and Running*, in aid of the Injured Jockeys Holiday Fund.

There are a lot of self-appointed animal physios around nowadays, putting horses' backs right, a practice some old-fashioned trainers don't believe in. A few years ago, we had a man come to the yard who would never let us see him treat the horses. He would go into the box with the horse and close the door behind him. He did plenty of grunting and a bit of slapping. Then he would come out and say, 'That's put him right. It's a good job I came when I did. He was all wrong. He will improve lengths after that.' The same 'faith-healer' went to see a broodmare at a small stud owned by two sisters. Again, he suggested they wait outside while he treated the horse. He didn't realise that the box was rigged with close-circuit TV to monitor the mares when foaling. Of course, the sisters go and switch on the system which relays the picture to their kitchen. Yer man has a look in the manger, possibly to see if the mare has eaten up, sniffs the hay in the rack, has a piss in the corner of the box and lets off some wind. Then he has a look at the mare, gives her a couple of pats on her neck and a few slaps on her hindquarters, comes out and says to the ladies, 'She'll be better for that. You shouldn't have any more trouble with her now, but I will pop in next time I am passing to make sure.'

9

A Proud Moment for Mikey

It's just two days before the Flat starts. Today is the first day our Saab sponsorship sheets have been put on our horses to exercise in. The colours are red, white and blue, with the silver Saab logo, and look absolutely brilliant on the horses. And our cars are out off this world.

It's nice to have super motors around us although, I must confess, it wasn't always the case. The first car that I owned was a Morris Oxford so ancient it still had running boards. It was fifteen years old when I bought it from Tommy Lynch's father-in-law, Percy Craft, who was about to buy a new car. Tommy was a paid lad at Charlie Hall's when I

Tommy Lynch, not only posing with Betsy, but also posing as a soldier for a laugh

Percy Craft, Tommy Lynch and JB

was an apprentice there. It took about a week to do the deal with Mr Craft. It wasn't so much the money, but whether I was a fit person to own the car. Mr Craft treated Betsy, as he affectionately called her, with special care. She always looked immaculate and every Sunday he spent most of the day cleaning and polishing the old girl and wouldn't dream of taking her out in the rain. I ended up giving Tom's in-law thirty pounds for her and a faithful promise to look after her.

A year or so before I became the proud owner of Betsy, I had gone fishing one Sunday afternoon with Tommy, his bride-to-be Doreen and Mr and Mrs Craft. Mr Craft made us all get out, including his missus, and walk the half-mile or so down to the river as he said it was too rough on Betsy with us all inside and he didn't want to hurt her springs.

I heard on the grapevine later on that Mr Craft had seen me driving Betsy and considered I had been travelling too fast; if he ever caught me, he said, he would kick my arse. Ten days after I had bought Betsy, I drove to Flaxton Moor to do a bit of work on Markeast, a jumper I rode in races for Tom Walker, a permit trainer. On the return journey I was passing a bike on the road parallel with York racecourse when a car coming from the other direction wiped me out. What a mess Betsy looked with half her face all bashed-in and water pouring out from under her bonnet, just as if the poor bitch was crying. She was beyond repair but after several pit-stops for me to give her a drink, I just managed to limp home. I sold her to a scrapman in Sherburn-in-Elmet for eight pounds and dodged Mr Craft until the day I left Towton.

Markeast was a great little mare for me as she ran every week. In those days, the riding fee was about seven guineas. One could draw it at the scales after the race from the Weatherbys man, which I often did. After paying the valet his one-pound charge, helped with the petrol of whichever jockey I had scrounged a lift from, then stopped for a meal on the way home, my wages nowhere near covered my costs.

Our secretary, Helen, has just brought me in one of my personal cheques to sign for half the cost of Jo's Ascot gear that I promised I would pay for as a birthday present. Phew! It's a good job I was sat down. I doubt that I will be so generous next year, especially if I am to retire.

Which reminds me of the tale of a village couple who had just retired. The old boy said to his good lady, 'Now that we have retired, we will have to go a bit steady with the money to make it last out.' 'Nah, lad, you've no need to worry on that score. If you remember, every time we made love, I charged you a few bob.' 'Yes I do,' he replied. 'Well, with all the money you gave me, I saved up and every time one of that row of cottages came up, I bought it. We get a good income from the rents and if you hadn't been so lazy on a Sunday, we would have owned the shop on the corner as well!'

It all starts today, 25 March 1999, the opening of the new Flat season. At 7.25 a.m. I was interviewed on Radio Four. Half an hour later, I had the pleasure of having another chat on Radio Five with Cornelius Lysaght. Would you believe it, when I got to Doncaster, I was asked to say a few words for Radio Leeds and do a slot for Yorkshire Television.

I then went to the get-together for the Lincoln draw and had a bit of crack with David O'Leary, the manager of my football team, Leeds

Fran Marshall with JB and cheque

United, as David was drawing out the horses' names and letting the connections choose their own draw. This is the second year of this idea and I must say it adds a bit of spice to the race. Steve Huison, who plays Lumper in *The Full Monty*, officiated last year – with his clothes on. The highlight of the day was when Fran Marshall presented me with a cheque for twelve thousand pounds in the winner's enclosure for the Injured Jockeys Holiday Fund – the proceeds of Ken Oliver's eighty-fifth-birthday bash at Kelso.

Unfortunately, our Brocklesby runner, Paris Star, couldn't get us off to a flyer. Singsong, by Paris House out of Miss Whittingham, became our first two-year-old winner of the season when taking the Grey Friars under John Carroll on the third day of the meeting. Paris House won the same race first time out in 1991 and Miss Whittingham won five races for us. We bred Singsong and Miss Whittingham is now in foal to Mind Games, whom we also trained, so you could say that we are keeping it in the family.

71

I have no intention of taking over from Chris Evans, Michael Parkinson or anybody else. In fact the punters must have been fed up with listening to me on the radio or watching me on TV. But I'm afraid they had to listen to me spouting yet again on the Racing Channel, following Singsong's victory.

When I was a gunner in the King's Troop RHA, the day of the Royal Artillery Gold Cup was always an event to look forward to because we got the chance of a rare day off. In fact, transport from St John's Wood was even laid on to take us to Sandown to watch the race, free of charge. Never in my wildest dreams did I ever expect to have a runner in the race, let alone train the winner, which is what happened on the second to last day of March, when Carlisle Banditos did the business, ridden by Lieutenant Alex Michael.

Along with Wiltshire trainer Mikey Heaton-Ellis, who also served in the King's Troop, I have leased a horse to run in the Cup for most of the past seven years. In 1992 we won with Camden Belle, ridden by Major Ollie Ellwood and owned by Menin Muggeridge. Most of the other horses that we have leased have been moderate. In fact, for some of them you would have needed the telescope from Jodrell Bank to spot them in the distance, but at least we had the interest of being involved.

The Royal Artillery Gold Cup has been on the go since 1920, when Curraghour won. In 1958, Spittal Hill won the race, ridden by Captain C. D. Thatcher, the officer for whom I was groom while in the troop.

This year, Chris and Antonia Deuters kindly leased their half share of The Bandit to Mikey, who proudly received the Gold Cup presented to him by the Queen Mum, while I leased my half to Antonia's brother, Lieutenant-Colonel Angus Taverner. On teletext, the write-up said, 'Alex Michael produced a polished effort, crouching stylishly in the saddle in a similar fashion to Frankie Dettori.'

I had originally tried to get Ollie Ellwood to ride The Bandit but he was committed to last year's winner, Magnetic Reel, who, would you believe, we trained as a two-year-old. Ollie told me that Alex rode well and had ridden some point-to-point winners. A few days before the race, I invited Alex down to the yard to sit on The Bandit. Alex went with our other two jumpers, Amlwch and Smolensk, for about nine

PHOTOGRAPH: MARY PITT

*Carlisle Banditos ridden by Lieutenant Alex Michael winning
the Royal Artillery Gold Cup*

furlongs. He was very stylish and able to claim a very valuable seven
pounds. I just hoped this fellow wasn't that pro Angel Jacobs, making
another comeback posing as an amateur. That's all we need!

Mikey took a serious fall at Huntington races a few years ago, which
left him in a wheelchair. As if that's not bad enough, he has since been
afflicted with cerebral palsy. It was specially gratifying for Mikey to
receive the trophy from the Queen Mum.

Carlisle Banditos travelled on his own to Sandown but returned with
company, a chocolate-brown labrador pup I bought from my old pal
Garry Blum's son Martin, who delivered him to our horse-box. There
are no prizes for guessing the pup's name – Bandit.The following day
Alex's riding was all the rage and no end of folk rang me to ask where I
got my jockey from, including jump trainer David Nicholson and Grand
National-winning jockey Bob Champion.

Nowadays, our yard isn't associated with training jumpers, although

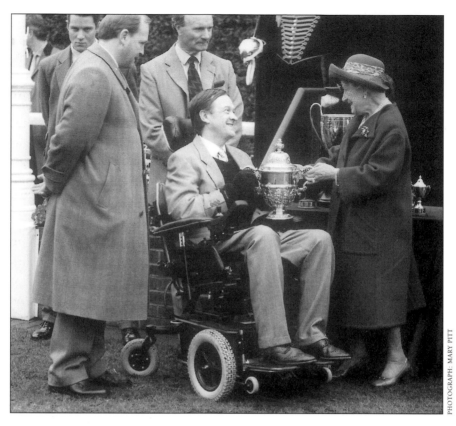

PHOTOGRAPH: MARY PITT

*Queen Elizabeth the Queen Mother presenting the Royal Artillery Gold
Cup to winning owner Mikey Heaton-Ellis*

we started with them. Before we put the all-weather gallops down, the
jumpers needed miles of long, steady work, so we used to box four
horses at a time and take them down to Fluke Hall Beach, about five
miles away. One of our lads had been away on his weekend off and
came back with ugliest face-mask you ever did see. It was absolutely
grotesque. For a laugh, I borrowed it next time I drove down to the
beach. When we came to the very narrow shore road, a Land-Rover and
cattle trailer came into view. I quickly donned the mask. We had to go
steady to pass. The lady driver looked at me and got such a fright that
she almost went through the hedge. On the beach were four or five
council men excavating with diggers, loading sand up into a wagon.

They stopped while we walked by on our way to the galloping area. I was leading the string on our chaser, Duffle Coat, wearing the mask. As we rode past, one of the men said, 'That's Jack Berry in front!'

On 3 April, we had the pleasure of welcoming the North-West Racing Club to our yard, on a lovely warm sunny day. As Saturday is our work day, the club members enjoyed a good bit of action. First, we worked seven pairs of two-year-olds. I mounted my quad bike, as I wanted to see the horses at the other end of the gallops. Some of the punters got so close to the running rail they could have stroked the horses as they passed, but the youngsters just flew by without batting an eyelid.

June Hobart, an old lady equipped with a stick, from Alderley Edge in Cheshire, couldn't lay up with rest. Even Stevie Wonder could see she was lagging behind. I did a bit of whipping-in and managed to get her loaded on my quad bike. She loved the experience and saw far more of the horses than the others. A few days later a lovely card arrived in the post from Mrs Hobart telling me she had had a fantastic day and it was her first ride on a bike for over sixty years.

Following a tour of the yard, the members had coffee and biscuits in our house, then went on either to Flat racing at Haydock or jumping at Carlisle. Our couple of runners at Haydock ran well enough without getting into the frame. Jo and I were invited to lunch in the box belonging to Terry and Margaret Holdcroft, owners of the Bearstone Stud. I had to be very careful eating as I had a tooth come off my bottom plate during the meal and very nearly swallowed it. Trying to eat and put the tooth back in without anyone noticing was a work of art but I managed it somehow.

The next day, I went to the dentist to have the tooth stuck back. I fully appreciate the national minimum wage came into force on the 1 April at three sixty an hour; I can live with that. But to take two minutes to stick the tooth back in and have me sit in the waiting-room for ten minutes whilst the glue dried and then to charge thirty-two pounds twenty-five pence – I thought that was bit steep.

Shane Kitching, our equine dentist, works his butt off, rasping horses' teeth and pulling out wolf-teeth (which can take up to half an hour), to justify his twenty-pound charge.

75

10

Tenerife, Here We Come

The horses are running a bit up and down at the moment. We ran some nice two-year-olds on Easter Monday without success, although Garnock Valley, our only runner at Southwell, won yesterday, giving us our fourth winner in the first two weeks of the new season.

The next day, our two-year-old Welch's Dream was second in the first race at Ripon. I had to dash back to base straight after the race to be home before 5.00 p.m. as the vet was coming to scan It's All Relative, to make sure that she was in foal after her visit to Mind Games, and to scope a two-year-old that had run moderately at Warwick. On my return from Ripon, Sue in our office told me that one of our ex-lasses, Nicola Campion, had given birth to an 11lb 2oz baby girl by Caesarean. Not to be outdone Joanne, our housekeeper, chimes in: 'I needed stitches after my first baby weighed in at only 6lb 4oz – but there was a woman in the same ward who gave birth to a boy that weighed 15lb 3oz and she didn't have a Caesarean or any stitches!' When I went in the yard to see the vet scope the horses, I did not dare tell him what I had just heard until he had reeled the pipe out of the horse's throat, for fear of him choking the poor thing with laughing.

On Friday, the day before the Grand National, Lord Daresbury and the directors of Aintree kindly invited Jo and me to lunch, along with about a hundred or so other guests. At our table we enjoyed the company of the good lord's brother Johnny Greenall and his wife Laura, along with Willie and Caroline Jenks. Newbury trainer Charles Egerton came rushing in, very late, bedraggled and sweating like a bull, looking as if he had galloped a couple of circuits of the National course. I'm sure he would have felt a lot better had he called round to the stables and got one of his lads to hose him down.

At Aintree it was nice to see on the Racing Channel our two-year-old Paris Star shine when winning his maiden at Lingfield. Carlisle Banditos unfortunately pulled up lame in the Mumm Mildmay Chase and had to hitch a lift back in the horse ambulance. I must say, the Aintree vets were brilliant. No sooner had the horse stepped out of the ambulance than Dr Proudman and his Australian assistant were straight on to the case, soothing Bandit's leg with ice for fifteen minutes, strapping the leg up and injecting him with a painkiller and an anti-inflammatory. After settling him for the night at the racecourse stables, the vets arranged to visit him again at 7 a.m. The doom eased a little as we shouted Amlwch home in the novice chase at Sedgefield from the luncheon marquee.

In the evening, same as last year, I was invited to do a talk about the Injured Jockeys Holiday Fund at the Celebrity Sportsmen's evening at the George Hotel in Liverpool, arranged by the city's Lions Club. John Morgan of the *Yorkshire Post* was speaking, along with sports reporter Julian Armfield and ex-jockey Declan Murphy. Jockey and Racing Channel presenter Luke Harvey did a Grand National talk-in. The night went very well and earned quite a few pounds for several good causes.

On 14 and 15 April the final breeze-up sales of the season take place at Newmarket. As you would expect, I couldn't keep away, but I did manage to keep my hands in my pockets most of the time on the first night, although I was under-bidder on a Clantime colt I liked the look of. As ever, I stayed at the Blums' residence. To be honest, I think Mrs Blum must be losing her grip at the Jenga game, as I beat her yet again.

Unfortunately, our Royal Ascot winner Rosselli has had to go to Rossdale vets in Newmarket for X-rays and a leg-scan as his off-fore joint keeps swelling up. I visited Rosselli and chatted to the vets about the problem, for which they recommended one month's box rest.

City Index very kindly invited me for lunch and tea, where I was drawn next to Alex Ferguson. Whilst we were having tea, I mentioned to Alex about a very nice Lake Coniston colt I saw breeze in the morning, which he, too, liked the sound of. I said, 'If we buy him, are you game to take half of him, and I wouldn't mind asking David O'Leary, the Leeds manager, if he would like to be the proud owner of the other half.' Alex thought that a brilliant idea.

To be honest, I think Mrs Blum must be losing her grip at the Jenga game, as I beat her yet again.

Singsong, our Newmarket runner, ran a good race to finish third and I had the pleasure of watching the three-year-old filly, Angie Baby, owned by our Sam and his mates, win at Thirsk on SIS in the Tote credit shop. I would have watched Uncle Exact, our two-year-old, run from the Tote credit shop too, but I had left my binoculars, with my trainer's badge on them, in the luncheon marquee. It was only a minute until the off and the man on the gate to the members' entrance, a *Dad's Army* NCO lookalike, said, 'You can't come in here, Jack, without a badge.' To be honest, with him calling me Jack, I thought he was joking. But it was for real, even though I had already been in to watch an earlier race, so he knew I had a badge. Even the punters standing around were saying, 'Let him in, man, he wants to see a race.' After preparing Uncle Exact for weeks it was a bit niggling being denied the chance to see the horse run his first race by another case of 'I am only doing my job.'

At the breeze-up sales after racing, I managed to buy the Lake Coniston horse. I only need to get in touch with David now, and if he's game, I would love to call the horse Leeds U Man or Man U Leeds, but it will have to be put on hold until Wednesday as at five o'clock in the morning I am on my first leg by taxi to visit Tenerife with the injured jockeys for their annual holiday.

When we arrived in Tenerife, the airport lounge was packed and the taxi queue looked about two furlongs long. As I was waiting for a cab, Jack Hanson rang me on my yuppie to say that he had seen in the *Racing Post* that I had bought the Lake Coniston horse and he would like to take the half with Alex.

This year, among the runners on the holiday trip are Jimmy and Ann Harris, Fred and Diana Winter, Ronnie Sheather, Tommy and Pat Jennings, Frank and Val Dever, John and Linda O'Hara, Tommy and June Skuse, Sharron Murgatroyd, Con and Marrion Kenneally, Jeff Brooks, Jacqui Oliver, Kevin and Linda McCauley, Lex Kelly, Peter and Angela Hallas, Des Cullen, Mary Boulton, Jack and Betty Dowdeswell, Fred and Isa Cheshire, Paddy and Nan Broderick and a good few more, fifty-four in all, including carers.

The whole cost of the holiday this year was very kindly sponsored by the trustees of the R. G. Hills Charitable Trust, so that the £43,472 we have collected during the year will go towards next year's holiday. Ultimately, I would love to see the beneficiaries with their own place, funded by a consortium of sportspeople prepared to buy some land out here in Tenerife, where the climate is so good, and build a really modern complex for all victims of sports-related injuries and their loved ones to enjoy. It could be achieved if all sport's governing bodies paid something to get it off the ground, possibly with a grant from the lottery fund. A hotel with a beauty parlour and shops could be part of it and, in time, it would even make a profit.

Paddy Broderick was sharp and on the ball, just like in my day when he rode for W. A. Stephenson. First thing in the morning – I'm talking five or six in the morning – he was down at the pool with his towels to beat the Germans to the sunbeds. Jack Dowdeswell, at eighty-two, wasn't far behind. I bet it wasn't easy to get up Jack's inner when he was riding.

At Sunday night's evening meal the choice was spaghetti with prawns or roast lamb. When the prawns and the spaghetti were delivered to the table, finding a prawn amongst the spaghetti was as difficult as backing the winner of a Showcase handicap. I think the chef that made it must have been allergic to fish. When someone did find a prawn there was a rousing cheer which even the waiters joined in. Jack had put his order in for spaghetti. On viewing the dish when the waiter arrived with it for the first punters, he changed his mind and went for the lamb, leaving a spare prawn dish and lamb short. A big debate then ensued as to who had originally ordered the prawns.

What a cracking evening we had, some dancing, others doing wheelies in their chairs. The following night we were all invited to David Beddis's bar at Sandblast, which is a twenty-minute drive from the Mary-sol complex where we stay. David, the son of one of our owners who had that good horse Clantime, very kindly put on a barbecue for us. In addition David staged an auction. One of the items on offer was the red shirt on my back, along with a raffle. On our return, we changed the pesetas back into sterling, netting another nine hundred and ninety-five pounds for the holiday fund.

Sharron Murgatroyd broke her neck in a fall from a horse in a race at Bangor-on-Dee in 1991. I salute Sharron's bravery. In appreciation of the help and treatment she received from the hospital that cared for her, she arranged a wheelchair push from the scene of the accident to the hospital where she was treated and raised no less than forty thousand pounds for the hospital. Not satisfied with that, she asked me if I could arrange for her to do a ten-thousand-feet tandem parachute jump for the Injured Jockeys Holiday Fund on our open day. Jonathon Haynes, who is also in a wheelchair, from a racing accident at Southwell in 1980, performed a parachute jump for us in 1983, when we raised a hundred and thirt-one thousand pounds for the International Spinal Research Trust. I might also add that that year Geraldine Rees, the Lancashire trainer, did a sponsored bungee jump for the same cause.

Back in England, PriceWaterhouseCoopers held a lunch at Beverley races. I was seated next to my old jockey pal, Jimmy FitzGerald. Jimmy

Jo and Sharron Murgatroyd in Tenerife

asked me if I had seen the front page of that day's *Racing Post*, which reported the deaths of Tim Forster, at the age of sixty-five, and of fifty-nine-year-old Paul Kelleway. Both died from cancer having recently retired from training. Paul's racing life spanned forty years as a jockey and a trainer. He trained seven Group 1 winners, having ridden Bula to victory in the Champion Hurdle and What a Myth to win the Cheltenham Gold Cup. Tim trained the winner of just about every decent steeplechase in the calendar, including three Grand National winners.

'You are too young to retire,' says Jimmy. 'When you take it easy and stop getting hassle and aggravation, the feet curl up.' I remember Ian Balding telling me last year that he would like to retire but no one seems to live very long afterwards when they do. I hope it's not true.

Would you believe its Saturday, 24 April and today is the first time we have been able to work the horses on grass, on account of the grass gallops being so wet. The two-year-olds loved it and I am sure that they will benefit from the experience. Our youngsters are behind from previous years, due to the wet and cold weather, but if we get a few more warm and sunny days, like today, the horses will be seen winning from all angles as we have some real nice sorts.

Walter Gott, who sadly had a car accident years ago which put him in a wheelchair, came to see his quarter share of Four Men (remember, I sold him in Barbados). Walter came to the yard with a couple of mates called Jeff and Lawrence. They told us about the time the three of them arrived back at their hotel after a night out on the town. Jeff is used to dealing with Walter's wheelchair but Lawrence is a bit of a novice. They had to negotiate the steps with Jeff pulling the chair backwards, holding the handles, and Lawrence taking the weight at the foot-plate. As they reached the third step, the handles came off the chair. Walter and the chair fly down the steps, run over Lawrence, who is trying to get out of the way but falls flat on his back, getting run over by Walter, who by then is going like stink and well out of control. Amazingly, Walter is still upright in the chair which is heading for a low wall with surrounding shrubbery and a pond in the middle. The chair hits the wall and Walter is catapulted into the pond, where he lies cursing and swearing. Fellow guests rush to the rescue – but they are German and don't speak

SAAB   ***SAAB PRESS RELEASE.***

TAKE IT AS "RED " JACK !

The SAAB sponsorship of Jack Berry's racing stable included a top of the range car for the popular trainer and one for his wife Jo.

Both were gratefully accepted but Jack saw " Red" and asked for a vehicle in his favourite colour.

*He will pick up the car at **REDCAR** races on Thursday April 29th and receive the keys to the SAAB special after the first race.*

Jack said: " The car is available in silver and black. But red has been my favourite colour from way back.

"Everyone knows that I wear lucky red shirts and have red in my racing colours. " Jack quipped " When I first started training even my bank balance was in the red. "

Redcar Racecourse is the appropriate venue for the presentation and the Manager and Clerk of the Course John Gundill said: " We are delighted that SAAB and Jack chose the opening day of our 1999 Flat season for this ceremony.

"Jack is a good friend to racing and he has always supported Redcar.

Jack retires from training at the end of the current campaign and he will hand over the reins of Moss Side Stables, Cockerham, Lancaster, to his son Alan.
Jack said" I will still be in touch and offering help but Alan is 35 and has earned his chance. "

Jack has trained over 1,500 winners and he was awarded the M.B.E for his services to races and various charities.

He said " I motor between 55,000 and 60,000 miles a year and the SAAB will make driving easier and more comfortable.
" My first car cost £30. It was a 15 year old Morris
Ten days later I crashed

Jack has a warning for punters. He said; " We have made a slower start than usual to the season. This is due to the wet winter, which was more suitable to sea horses than my two-year-olds. In another week or two they will be flying.

" Ninety Degrees, One Domino, Paris Star and Cautionary are juveniles to follow.

" I must also put in a good word for Red Sun, Red King and Red Typhoon. They belong to the Red Shirt Brigade."

Jack added, " We want to make this season one to remember with lots of winners. Then I will have more time to devote to my hobbies, watching soccer and cricket. Above all I will be able to enjoy my SAAB – a little red gem – like me!

SAAB executive Ian Hutchinson said " We have strong associations with horse racing and sponsor Henry Cecil's stable, and jockeys Richard Dunwoody, Kieren Fallon and Willie Ryan.

"We are delighted to have Jack on board. He is fine ambassador for the sport. "

JB's new Saab

English. They mistakenly pick Lawrence up, put him in Walter's chair and cart him off to reception to get help. Meanwhile, Walter is still in the pond and Jeff is at the top of the steps, wheelchair handles in hands, tears rolling down his face, as Walter yells at him to 'bring my effing wheelchair back and get me out of the water!'

Today, Thursday, 29 April, not only did Persian Fayre win for us at Redcar, but, as you can see from the press-release, it was also the day I took over my red Saab, which I can assure you is some machine.

11

The Gallop That Failed

Saturday, 1 May. What a great surprise I got today via a phonecall from Lord Oaksey, telling me the late Tim Forster had left the Injured Jockeys Holiday Fund something in his will. I couldn't believe my ears when he told me it was a staggering twenty-five thousand pounds.

The following morning the manager of Manchester United Football Club came to the yard just before 8.00 a.m., mainly to get away from his working environment and see his horses – and have a bacon sandwich at Jack's café. Alex saw for the first time his fifty per cent of the Lake Coniston two-year-old, which John Carroll came to ride a canter. One of our lads, Ian Pike, rode Ninety Degrees, Alex's other youngster, later in the day.

The same day, our well-bred two-year-old Cautionary won at Hamilton, which leaves our yard only one to go to reach the sixteen-hundred-winner mark. On my return from Hamilton, Grace Harper, a lady who has a share in the Red-Shirt Brigade, whose late husband Norman owned horses with us in the past but sadly died a couple of years ago, rang me to say that she had been looking forward to seeing Red Typhoon running at Redcar tomorrow but unfortunately she wouldn't be able to be there as she has to go into hospital to have a mastectomy. Usually I can talk my way through anything but I just didn't know what to say on this occasion and she appeared to be so brave about it all. Eventually, I said how sad I was to hear this news, to which Grace replied, 'At least I will lose a bit of weight.' To brighten up her day the girls in the office sent Grace a bunch of flowers.

There was no fairy-tale win for Grace, though, with Red Typhoon at Newcastle. Although she went off in the race at 5–2 favourite, the filly only ran well enough to finish fourth of eighteen under Paul Fessey.

The following day, we had a nice change of fortune, winning the first two races at Hamilton. Peter's Imp, beautifully ridden by the leading lady rider, Emma Ramsden, took the six-furlong amateurs' race to give us our sixteen-hundredth winner. Our two-year-old Uncle Exact followed at cramped odds of 1–3. Unfortunately, I wasn't there as I had arranged to be at Chester at 11.30 a.m. to do a little brown-envelope job for the Racing Channel. Although things happen very quickly round Chester, I fancied our two-year-old Medina de Rioseco in a major way, but she could only finish third to the useful Harryana.

The following day, Lady Luck was thankfully still with us, as John Carroll teamed up with the old firm to win the first two races at Carlisle with our débutante two-year-old Brave Burt and Persian Fayre. On the first day of Chester, I was invited to lunch before racing by Joseph Heler whose Cheshire Cheese Company used to sponsor the yard. I had to sing for my supper by giving a rundown on the horses and making some selections for the benefit of Joe's business associates and friends. I selected Housemaster in the Victor Chandler Chester Vase which duly obliged at 8–1, only to be disqualified and placed fourth. King Darius made amends with a 7–1 win before my each-way selection, Zaragossa, finished third at 12–1.

Talk about jockeys riding at two meetings being a bit rough on them, and them having bad days – but what about The Bride? She took a bit of a beating on Saturday, 8 May. Starting at home, she drove to Lingfield, where she tacked up Bon Ami to finish eighth of twenty in the feature race. On her way home, she dived into Warwick to see Amlwch, usually a good jumper, refuse in the novice chase.

It was then on to Wolverhampton, where she saddled up the 5–2 favourite, Tuscan Dream, in the sprint. He bolted to the start and finished second last.

It may seem a bit hard on the old girl, but at least it kept her out of the shops. Don't feel too sorry for Jo. She's tough. Years ago I broke my leg in a fall at Wetherby. At the time the kids were very young and we took them to Butlins holiday camp at Skegness during my convalescence. The redcoats were brilliant and did all sorts to entertain and get the campers involved. One afternoon they staged ladies' boxing bouts

Jo Berry – The Bride

at various weights and my missus volunteered. She was prancing round the ring in her shorts and gloves looking like a miniature Jap Stam, and they couldn't find an opponent to take her on at any price!

On the Monday, our twelve-year-old soldier Amron, ridden by Paul Bradley, showed the other twenty-nine starters the way home at Redcar. When the old chap came back into training this year, Flash said to me, 'Isn't it time we roughed Ronnie off as we mentioned last season?' But Roy Peebles, his owner, decided to put him back into training and retire him if he didn't enjoy it.

Being realistic, who has the best life, Ronnie or Ollie (O. I. Oyston)? Ronnie lives in the front yard and sees everything that goes on. The staff pass him a thousand times a day, say hello, pat him and stuff him with Polos. He is ridden out for an hour or so each day, has two or three little trips on the gallops weekly, and every day after lunch he is turned out in a paddock. In fact he has the life of Riley at Cockerham. In the off-season, we send him up to Sarah Cousins livery yard for his holidays.

Ollie, the winner of twenty-four races, is now twenty-three years old and lives in a nice sheltered three-acre paddock with a big double stable for shelter with his pony friend, Barney Rubble. Both get well fed at either end of the day. Ollie has good rugs on him in winter, is wormed every month, shod in front and has regular foot trims. He has his annual Prevac tetanus injection from the vet, Shane the dentist rasps his teeth every year and we all love the old fellow something rotten. As has been well documented, Ollie is the only thing I wouldn't sell.

I used to ride him on our open day for years after he retired from racing at twelve years old. To get him ready for the event, I rode him out every day for a month or so beforehand for fear of him getting too excited and throwing a wobbler. It took him a month in his paddock to settle down again afterwards. He would have loved to have carried on racing. In view of that, I think Ronnie is the better off. But which of the two has the better life is really irrelevant. One thing is certain. These old gentlemen, and a few more now on the verge of retirement at Moss Side Racing Stables, won't be going to any sales or anywhere else for that matter when their racing careers are over. They have served us well and will stay put, here, or wherever I go, until the end.

On Friday, 14 May, following the success of Mamma's Boy at Thirsk, I went to Tony Fawcett's house to change into my monkey suit as that night I was auctioneer at the Norton and District Lions Club for a sportsmen's dinner in aid of the Injured Jockeys Holiday Fund and the Camphill Village Trust in Malton, which cares for physically and mentally disadvantaged people. There was a very good turnout from the racing crowd. My old pal John Morgan, Lorcan Wyer and Les Eyre were the celebrity guests. We had a very good night and raised over eight thousand pounds.

Let me say, there is no way we attend these charity functions just as dutiful do-gooders. We have some great laughs and it is a pleasure raising money for such good causes. For Question Time, paper and pens had been put on the tables for questions to be written down. Some were silly, some were quite good, but there were far too many for us to answer in one night.

One question put to Les Eyre was, 'Mick Easterby has this week in the *Racing Post*, described Flat jockeys as over-paid, cocky little buggers. What is your opinion?'

Lorcan had one directed at him from journalist Tom O'Ryan, 'Roughly how far round is Market Rasen racecourse and how do you pacify an irate Neville Callaghan?' (Lorcan misjudged the winning-post one day when riding for Neville!)

I was asked about my most embarrassing moment. The questioner probably thought I would say the evening meeting at Hamilton, when we mixed up the races for Perigeux and Royal Dream, but it wasn't. I had one worse than that.

A question to Les was, 'What was Lester Piggott's lightest weight?' The Hambleton handler got it spot on with, 'I suppose about 8lb 2oz, when he was born!'

Lorcan had to field the rudest question of the evening, 'Have you ever jumped a fence and s**t yourself?'

To enable Alan to pass all the relevant trials and tests to train, he went on Sunday, 16 May to the Racing School at Newmarket for the first of three separate courses. Each course costs in the region of eight hundred pounds, so the financial outlay is not trifling and may even deter would-be trainers from taking part. At the other end of the scale, because this system was only introduced in December of last year, the cost may have pushed permit holders and young hopefuls to take out a licence prematurely, without full business knowledge, in order to avoid paying for the course.

The seminars lasted all day and covered every aspect of running a successful business, from contracts, accounts, VAT, PAYE, taxation, budgeting, cash-flows, marketing – the list was endless. The June course covers staff management. (I don't want to be labelled a staff-knocker, as I started from the bottom myself and nobody is perfect, but to get staff nowadays to pay attention to such things as keeping their bungalows nice and tidy is not easy. And if someone does something really silly, like leaving a tap on all night or a horse tied up, try finding the culprit! You wouldn't get a result if you called in Sherlock Holmes. All you get is, 'Wasn't me.' I once named a horse Wasn't Me. Oh, and the hostel – some days, even Kate Adie would refuse to go in there. Joking apart, staff problems are the worst part of our job.) The June session also covers hours, health and safety, and office management. (Thankfully, I have a good office staff to look after all these things. I wouldn't know how to switch the computer on, but I am great on the phone, through plenty of practice.) The third and final part in July deals with racehorse management and covers sales procedures, horse health, feeding, nutrition, training and fitness, licensing and racecourse procedures.

Much as I would have liked to, I had no chance of going to Wembley to watch Manchester United beat Newcastle 2–0 in the FA Cup Final. Not only did I not have a ticket, but we had runners at Catterick in the afternoon and at Wolverhampton and Musselburgh in the evening. By choosing to go to Catterick, where our Lunch Party won, I could get home to watch a recording of the match on Sky at 8.00 p.m. and also watch our horses on Sky from Musselburgh and listen on the Racecall phone line to Wolverhampton, where Tuscan Dream completed an across-the-card treble, following Mamma's Boy's win at Musselburgh.

Paul Fessey, who went with me to Catterick, rode in the last race at 4.40 p.m. Just as we were about to get on to the M6, travelling at eighty-seven mph, we were pulled up by a lawman in an unmarked car. Although the car was my sponsored job, our lightweight jockey was doing the driving while I was riding shotgun, swotting up on the entries. Paul picked up a forty-pound fine and three points. It would have softened the blow if Paul had ridden Lunch Party, but, unfortunately for him, the horse was ridden by John Carroll.

Sifting through the stack of mail on my return from Catterick, I found the 'vet's certificate' I had told Sharron she would need to do the parachute jump at our open day. Sharron, you're a star!

Today – Sunday, 23 May – we had the pleasure of welcoming around forty members of the Laurel Racing Club on a stable visit to see their horse, Laurel Prince, and enjoy a buffet in our indoor school. The club

THE ROOKERY MEDICAL PARTNERSHIP

L A L BAXTER MB, BChir, DObst RCOG
E GLASBY MB, ChB, MRCGP, DRCOG
R J LONGMAN MB, BCh, MRCGP, DRCOG, DCH
M R SLOWE MB, BS, MRCGP, DRCOG
KUMAR SRISKANDAN MB, BCh, MRCGP, DRCOG, DCH
M WACE MA, MB, BChir, MRCGP, DRCOG
A J S WHITE MA, MB, BChir, MRCP, FRCGP, DCH
B C WIGGINS MA, BM, BCh, FRCSE
T D WILSON MB, ChB, MRCGP

ROOKERY MEDICAL CENTRE
NEWMARKET
SUFFOLK CB8 8NW

Telephone: (01638) 665711
Appointments: (01638) 664338
Fax: (01638) 561280

18 May, 1999

TO WHOM IT MAY CONCERN

Re Sharron MURGATROYD
Becklyn
Bury Road
Kennett

Dear Sir

re   Sharron MURGATROYD (d.o.b. 5.2.60)

I examined this girl, who is tetraplegic following an injury to her cervical spine several years ago after race-riding. She is I understand going to do a parachute jump in tandem with a trained instructor, at the beginning of August. She tells me that she needs a letter from her doctor to confirm that she is fit to do this from the point of view of her heart and lungs.

When I saw her today, she was looking well. Her blood pressure was 140/85. Her pulse 72 per minute, regular. Heart sounds were normal and chest was clear.

I expressed a slight concern regarding her cervical spine injury and the potential for a hard landing, but she assured me that she had spoken to her orthopaedic specialist, who had said that he saw no particular problem with it, and also the people with whom she was doing the parachute jump had been trained and had taken tetraplegics for parachute jumps before. Apart from her cervical spine injury, therefore, I find her otherwise fit and well.

Yours sincerely,

Dr Kumar Sriskandan

KS / SS

is winding down now since Andrew Hoyle, the boss, had a stroke in 1997. Laurel Racing Club used to be quite formidable, owning such prolific winners as Surrey Dancer, Majed, Palacegate Touch and, of course, Laurel Queen. During the club's seven years of racing horses, its members have had the pleasure of shouting home an incredible ninety-two winners.

The 'To Let' notice will have to go on Paris Star's door tonight. Paris Star was bought for Charlie Sparrowhawk at Tattersalls Fairyhouse Sales in Ireland for sixteen thousand guineas. He was very sharp early on, but of late he has tended to duck in behind horses during his races and we were not getting the best from him. I told Charlie the horse needs a confidence booster, as I hate putting blinkers on two-year-olds; we both agreed to put Paris Star in a claimer for ten thousand pounds at Hamilton on Monday, 24 May, a very quiet racing day. With only three horses in the race and just a small crowd in attendance, I didn't think anyone would bother putting in a claim for the horse.

Little did I know there would be a French trainer at the meeting looking for horses to run in France. With such moderate opposition, the race looked like a penalty kick for Paris Star. And so it proved. Starting the 4–5 favourite, Paris Star jumped off in front and had no trouble shaking off his two moderate rivals by a cosy two and a half lengths and fifteen lengths. Sure enough, a good-looking young lady, by the name of Madame Maurier, accompanied by a very slim Frenchman, put in a claim for the horse.

On behalf of Charlie, I lodged a friendly claim, only to lose on the ballot. I felt like saying, let's have the best of three, as I genuinely liked the little horse. With a name like Paris Star, by Paris House, it shouldn't be difficult for the trainer to find an owner for him in France.

Mind you, I didn't think anyone would put in a claim for Echo-Logical at Ayr on 25 July 1992. But someone did, on behalf of Peter Savill. At the time I was finding it hard to win with the horse as he was high in the handicap, so I entered him in the Ayr claimer with a price tag of twenty thousand pounds. For years, we had trained for Peter with a lot of success, but I had rattled his cage when he wanted me to train ten or so of his yearlings, which would all have been ridden by his retained jockey, Kevin Darley. Kevin is a great jockey and I like him a lot, but out of loyalty to our stable jockey, John Carroll, I declined to take the horses, reasoning that as John had a wife and two youngsters to support, it wasn't fair to take ten per cent of the yard's rides away from him. From that day forward, Peter had a pop at any decent horse I ran in a claimer, including Raggerty in 1993 and Jimmy the Skunk in 1994. We all know the rules, but often we run horses in claimers we would rather not get claimed. It's a risk you take. On the whole we are trying to nick soft races, but sometimes we come unstuck. I had to chuckle when I read a report in the *Racing Post* recently which quoted Peter Savill, after a clear-the-air breakfast meeting with Levy Board Chief Rodney Hughes, saying : 'We had a perfect meeting. We're not the sort to bear grudges.'

On Wednesday, 27 May, our day started desperately. Martel, one of our two-year-olds, was doing a piece of work and unfortunately fractured a pastern and had to be put down by our vet. Thankfully, he was the first work casualty we have had for over two and a half years, which, considering we have around a hundred horses in work most of the time, is not a bad average. Nevertheless, one fatality damps down the spirit of the yard. However, in the evening the sun shone again when our two-year-old, Welch's Dream, owned by David Hall and ridden by Frankie Dettori, won the maiden at Ripon.

It was a work of art trying to watch Manchester United versus Bayern Munich live from Bacelona on the TV screens at Ripon in between saddling up our four runners. The Germans had been leading one nil with only three minutes of extra time to go when Teddy Sherringham swept the ball home off a pass from Ryan Giggs. In the very next minute, a corner from David Beckham was flicked on to the other sub, Ole Gunnar Solskjaer, who had only been on the pitch a few minutes, and he booted the ball home. For Manchester United to score two goals in the last three minutes of injury time was sensational. The next day I rang Alex on his mobile to say, 'Well done!' only the operator on the answering service said, '*@?* ?*$!' meaning he wasn't there.

No wonder! I bet he had some headache celebrating winning the last leg of the magnificent cup treble. According to some reports United

Cath Ferguson with Jack Berry and the magnificent treble trophies

were lucky as the Germans hit the woodwork twice in the second half and but for a few inches the result could have been different. 'If' is a small word with a big meaning (if my auntie had had some bits, she would have been my uncle). Never mind all those hard-luck stories, though, as I read the result it said Manchester United 2, Bayern Munich 1.

It's surprising when a person, a yard, a team or whatever, is doing a bit of good, how the media want to cover it from every possible angle. Two radio stations rang the yard to ask me what Alex Ferguson is like. 'Is he as aggressive off the football scene as he is on it?' 'Does he talk about football or horses when he comes to the yard?' I'll let them into a secret. When he does come, I have never seen him once chewing gum to soothe the nerves, as he seems to do when we see him on TV at work.

What do you think of the letter and cartoon I received the other day, from an eighty-four-year-old retired schoolmaster.

Today, we had a runner at Sandown in one of my favourite races, the Group 2 Temple Stakes, which we won with Paris House in 1993, Mind

0151 – 652 – 1293

RICHARD SMITH
11t Grosvenor Rd.,
Birkenhead
CH43 1UB.

Dear Mr Berry,

I am a retired schoolmaster (84 on Tuesday) who has followed the horses since I was a lad. My father was a barber in Liverpool and my mother was Irish — possible influences?

When I married after the war I had a wife, five children and seven bookmakers to support on my basic teacher's salary — £189 a year when I started in London!! — so I was never able to have an interest in a horse. However, in 1981 I pulled off a quiet coup ante-post — Aldaniti at 25/1 in the National; Fairy Footsteps at 10/1 in the 1000 Gns and To-Agori-Mou at 6/1 in the 2000 so I had a few bob to invest.

I wrote to various trainers, yourself included, and eventually put my £1000 with Roger Fisher. No sooner had I committed myself than I had a

lovely letter from your wife with offers I inevitably had to turn down.

I have always deeply regretted this as the Fisher relationship proved utterly unsatisfactory and you, on the other hand, went from strength to strength. Such is fate!

I have never forgotten your wife's kind letter so I thought I would like to offer you this little cartoon I have done for you, with my very best wishes to you and your wife and the best of good fortune to your son when he takes over the shop.

Kindest regards

Yours sincerely,
Richard Smith

Games in 1995 and 1996 and Bolshoi in 1998. Instead of going there, however, I went to Redcar to see Blakey finish second, beaten by a neck. As a two-year-old Blakey was very weak and not good enough to sell on. I thought there was some good in him and rather than send him to the sales to fetch peanuts, we gave him three runs and turned him out to mature. Mark Johnston is a very talented trainer, but he is not the best at being sociable with other members of his profession. He only speaks when he feels like it, which is his prerogative, but as we all work together, sometimes it's nice to chat to one another. This is clearly not how Mark feels, and as the Middleham maestro reminded me so much of Blakey, the bus inspector from the TV series *On the Buses*, I named the horse Blakey in his honour.

Willie and Elaine Carson came to spend the evening and stay the night with us since the following day Willie and Claire Balding were filming our potential Ascot runners. After a meal at Bumbles restaurant, we went home to scan through old form books, looking up races to confirm we had given each other the right answers to races we were reminiscing over at dinner. Willie rode quite a number of winners for our yard during his career. One good horse he rode would be Clantime in 1983, when he won the Surrey Stakes on him at Epsom the day Teenoso won the Derby.

In beautiful sunshine, we had a great morning filming the horses working, watching them have a pick of grass and rolling in the sand-pit. This was followed by a brilliant, very relaxed and enjoyable chat in the house about horses past and present – only it went on for so long, I didn't get to go racing to Leicester or Redcar, where we managed a double with Peter's Imp and Antonia's Double.

June 2 was quite a busy day, and an eye-opener for Carol Heaton, a psychiatric nurse who had been given as a Christmas present A Day In The Life Of Jack Berry, would you believe. Carol duly arrived at 7 a.m. and watched us work seventy-two horses before we set off for Newcastle, in between taking dozens of phonecalls, answering lots of questions, giving orders and entering horses for races at Bath, Warwick and Pontefract with Alan. Fortunately Carol was a very fit lady and she kept up with me as I dashed about in between the lots of horses, although she will probably have sore shins in the morning! I thought she looked at me a bit strange when my missus gave us both a toasted teacake and a cup of tea as we crossed in the kitchen on the hoof; at that time of the morning there is no time to sit down to eat. Carol gave me the impression that she had been reading the articles by Sir Clement Freud in the *Racing Post*, where, more often than not, Clement has lavish, beautifully laid-out breakfasts with various trainers. At the races, the people that I didn't introduce Carol to probably thought that I had changed models, she kept so close.

Shinbone Alley started 4–7 favourite for the two-year-old maiden, but met a tartar in John Gosden's newcomer, Warm Heart. From the way he beat our man, this is by far the best youngster I have seen out this season; 'Ascot' was written all over him. There would have been plenty of burnt figures after Shinbone Alley's defeat, including those of a particular football manager who at the moment is on holiday with his wife Kath in the South of France, but it was well documented that Shinbone Alley was a good horse. Personally, I thought the horse was such a good thing that if I had been a big hitter, I would have burnt my fingers so badly that my missus would have had to clean my teeth and dress me every morning for weeks.

In the next race, I told viewers on the Racing Channel, when asked by Alex Hammond about Palacegate Jack's chances, that if he wanted, he could win by half the track, but as Jack is such an old villain (he would make Al Capone look like the Milky Bar Kid) he would do his own thing. For a welcome change, Jack held on in the race to win by the shortest of short heads; it was so close it took the judge twenty minutes to announce the result.

I was riding shotgun from Newcastle to the evening meeting at Chester with my old team mate John Carroll at the wheel. I told Carol to make sure she put a packet of Pampers in her bag before we set off. And that is all I am going to say about the ride to Chester, except that Carol was very quiet in the back! Because it had rained incessantly for twenty-four hours, making the going very soft, I didn't run La Caprice at Chester. She is a real nice filly and we want her to go to Ascot to run in the Queen Mary, so I dare not risk her in the soft. But we did run our

It's a dog's life in racing – waiting for the winners to come home

débutante filly, Susie's Flyer, a half-sister to our Wokingham winner, Selhurstpark Flyer, who got beat half a length by Richard Hannon's 2–5 shot, Watching. I was invited to be the Chester guest for Sky TV, which would have been a nice little earner, but unfortunately I could not get from Newcastle in time.

The following day, Carol brought a big bunch of flowers to the yard for Jo, and said she was absolutely worn out and did not know how on earth we kept going or when we managed to eat. (Which I though a bit off as when we arrived at Newcastle I had bought her a beef sandwich, and she had had that toasted tea-cake in the morning!)

Saturday, 5 June, Derby Day, saw us winnerless, although Bolshaya was close second at Doncaster. Unfortunately, I wasn't there as I was on duty at Haydock Park doing my little bit for the Flyde Junior RUFC and a promotion with our horse, French Connection, for Christie's cancer project. The RUFC auctioned a racing weekend at one of their fund-raising functions. Michael and Sheila Dickinson, along with their two friends, Keith and Shirley Nicolson, were the highest bidders this year.

They were picked up by a chauffeur-driven limousine, provided by Kwik-Save Tyres of Blackpool at 9.30 a.m. After a tour round, they arrived for lunch at the Ashfield House in Wigan, then on to Haydock races where the racecourse had very kindly left them four complimentary paddock badges. I gave them a tour round the paddock area and explained the racecard and betting to them. Fortunately, I managed to tip them three winners and the Derby winner, Oath, to boot, which they all backed. Following the racing they were floated off in the limo to St Anne's, as guests of the Grand Hotel, where they were shown to their rooms to relax before dinner. After breakfast at the hotel on Sunday, they were brought to Cockerham for a tour round the yard and a glass of champagne. Then it was on to Pilling for lunch and then home. They absolutely loved it. Although none of them had been racing before, they have caught the bug and are looking forward to going again, which can only be good for the game.

It's all go on our latest seven-furlong all-weather gallop at the moment, as we are having to take it all up. When we laid it last year it was absolutely brilliant. The material was plastic, heated up and made similar to three- to four-inch noodles, only between quarter to half an inch thick. When it was laid about six inches deep, on top of our polytrack, it all matted together creating a marvellous cushion with a rubbery texture for the horses to work on. The horses and riders loved it. There was no kickback whatsoever. In fact, it was like a mat and so good that I thought it would revolutionise all-weather surfaces. But over the winter months, with the cold and rain, the material perished and shrivelled up losing all its original texture. It then started to break down to a thickness of only half an inch or less, becoming very brittle and rubbing the horses' heals, making it impossible to use, even though the gallop material had had a five-year guarantee when we bought it for fifty-seven thousand pounds.

At the moment, we are getting no joy from the suppliers, Equitrack Limited. When we bought it, they assured us it had been tested in freezer-like conditions and, according to them, it was the dog's b*****ks! The same firm supplied Alan Jarvis and Graham McCourt with material for their gallops and theirs have subsequently gone the same way as ours. We have put Ian Bolland, our accountant, on the case to sort out the financial matters.

We have a hundred horses here, and we cannot wait. We need the gallop so we have to kick on and get rid of the useless stuff as best we can to enable us to put down a different surface in its place or top the gallop up with original stuff at our own expense. We have hired a contractor with a JCB to load wagons, tractors and trailers, which then head off in all directions, filling holes in fields, putting it on farm lanes and gateways, garden paths, indoor schools, anywhere and everywhere, just to get rid.

12

Goodbye, Old Friend

We get some great invitations to lunches and dinners in our profession. One in particular is the Timeform Charity Dinner, held at York Racecourse in the famous Gimcrack Rooms. Reg Griffin and Jim McGrath, directors of Timeform, stage this event annually in aid of Macmillan Cancer Relief and other charities. Since its inception in 1971, the charities have benefited by a staggering two and a half million pounds. And I must add that in recent years Timeform have very generously given our IJHF a substantial contribution.

The event took place on 11 June this year. The evening started with a toast to the Queen. A sumptuous dinner followed. Then Reg made a

J. Greenway, Esq	J. A. N. Prenn, Esq	S. E. Scrope, Esq	R. Tennant, Esq	B. P. Jenks, Esq	The Earl of Halifax	The Earl
Mrs R. Tennant	Mrs J. Greenway	Mrs J. A. N. Prenn	Lady Oaksey	Mrs S. E. Scrope	The Marchioness of Hartington	

Mrs J. F. Sanderson						
W. Newton, Esq	Mrs E. W. Davis	J. Sykes, Esq	P. Bilton, Esq	I. J. Blakey, Esq	Mrs N. Graham	C. F. Deuters, Esq
Mrs B. Yeardley	G. H. Leatham Esq	Mrs D. Oughtred	Mrs P. Shepherd	Ms S. Johnson	R. Whiteley, Esq	Mrs J. C. Smith
E. W. Davis, Esq	Mrs W. Newton	G. Reed, Esq	S. Curtis, Esq	L. McCormick, Esq	Mrs B. Phillips	D. Abell, Esq
Mrs G. H. Leatham	B. Yeardley, Esq	Miss S. McIntyre	Mrs J. L. Smith	Mrs G. C. W. Allan	N. Graham, Esq	Mrs M. Johnston
M. Grubb, Esq	Mrs R. Peebles	P. Shepherd, Esq	J. N. Gundill, Esq	B. Phillips, Esq	Mrs H. Moore	D. Wosskow, Esq
Mrs R. Aird	R. Aird, Esq	Mrs J. N. Gundill	Mrs H. Lott	Mrs L. McCormick	P. E. Robinson, Esq	Mrs R. Tindall
J. Berry, Esq	Mrs J. Berry	J. L. Smith, Esq	N. A. Blyth, Esq	G. C. W. Allan, Esq	Mrs N. J. Dawson	D. Lowrey, Esq
Mrs M. Grubb	R. Peebles, Esq	Mrs S. Curtis	Mrs G. Greetham	Mrs M. Wilson	H. Moore, Esq	Mrs E. Roseby
C. Lysaght, Esq	Mrs J. E. Tennant	H. Lott, Esq	J. G. Fitzgerald, Esq			M. D. Hammond, Esq
Mrs P. Murphy	P. Murphy, Esq	Mrs J. G. Fitzgerald	Mrs N. Cawthorne			Mrs E. Smith
J. E. Tennant, Esq		G. Greetham, Esq	N. Cawthorne, Esq			R. Leatham, Esq

short speech and introduced the main speaker, who this year was Professor Purdie. Rodney Tennant conducted the auction, realising forty-five thousand five hundred pounds from the seventeen lots donated by generous people.

The organisers also choose a Timeform Personality every year. In the past such names as Sir Peter O'Sullevan, Lester Piggott, Sir Noël Murless, Willie Carson, Dr Vincent O'Brien, John Francome, Peter Easterby, Jojo O'Neill, Martin Pipe, Lord Oaksey, Mark Johnson and Tony McCoy have been the recipients of this prestigious award.

Personally, I cannot understand why Reg Griffin, for all the work he has done for charities and the unselfish help he has given to others in raising money for good causes, hasn't been recognised with an official award, especially when one considers that I was awarded the MBE – for which I am extremely grateful and of which I am very proud – but don't think of myself as being in the same league as Reg. This year's personality was champion Flat jockey, Kieren Fallon, and, as the seating plan shows, there was a fair turnout with some quite notable people in attendance.

Cadogan	R. F. Griffin, Esq	Professor D. W. Purdie	The Marquess of Hartington	Colonel York	Lord Oaksey	The Marquess of Zetland
Mrs W. Sainer	The Countess Cadogan	The Countess of Halifax	Mrs C. St George	Mrs B. P. Jenks	Mrs E. C. York	Mrs R. D. Peacock
						J. F. Sanderson, Esq
Mrs C. F. Deuters	A. Turnell, Esq	Mrs J. Hollowood	R. Fahey, Esq	Mrs R. Merdith	H. H. Brown, Esq	Mrs J. O'Neill
J. M. Brown, Esq	Miss G. McHugh	P. Bourke, Esq	Mrs C. H. Stevens	C. H. Stevens, Esq	Mrs G. Crawford	J. C. McGrath, Esq
Mrs C. Shine	T. Holdcroft, Esq	Mrs R. Connew	R, Meredith, Esq	Mrs R. Fahey	J. O'Neill, Esq	Mrs H. H. Brown
J. C. Smith, Esq	Mrs T. Easterby	M. H. Easterby, Esq	Mrs P. J. Hodgetts	J. H. Williams, Esq	Mrs B. Gover	B. Gover, Esq
Mrs D. Abell	R. Connew, Esq	Mrs A. Arton	R. Freeston, Esq	Mrs H. Kaye	L. Cowburn, Esq	Mrs L. Cowburn
M. Johnston, Esq	Mrs P. Bourke	J. Hall, Esq	Miss E. Williams	P. J. Hodgetts, Esq	Mrs P. M. Lumb	D. W. Holdsworth, Esq
Mrs D. Lowrey	A. Arton, Esq	Mrs M. H. Easterby	H. Kaye, Esq	Mrs R. Freeston	M. J. B. Perkin, Esq	Mrs D. W. Holdsworth
R. Lindall, Esq	Mrs J. Gill	P. R. Bell, Esq	Mrs D. Hodgson	D. Hodgson, Esq	Mrs M. J. B. Perkin	
Mrs J. Uren	T. Easterby, Esq	Mrs I. Hall				
M. Leatham, Esq	Mrs T. Holdcroft	J. Gill, Esq				
Mrs M. D. Hammond	A. Belshaw, Esq	Mrs A. Belshaw				

All the winning connections for our Royal Ascot treble in the car park after racing: Jo Berry, Terry Holdcroft, Margaret Holdcroft, Jack Berry, Antonia Deuters, Chris Deuters, Trish Brown, David Brown.

This year's Royal Ascot was graced with lovely sunny weather every day. You may say that it is work, as we have runners there, but this is the one time of year that we push the boat out and stop at the Royal Berkshire Hotel – which costs an arm and a leg. The hotel was built in 1706 for Lady Anne Churchill, which makes it older then the racecourse itself. The house stayed in the Churchill family until 1846. In 1911 it was bought by the Horlick family of malted-drink fame, before passing to the Hoffmann family, who sold it to Ladbroke Hotels in 1985.

Unfortunately, at the Royal Meeting we only managed to get third with Brave Burt in the Norfolk, won by Warm Heart, the youngster

The Royal Ascot Treble:
Selhurstpark Flyer winning the Wokingham Stakes;
Bolshoi winning the King's Stand Stakes;
Rosselli winning the Norfolk Stakes

that had annihilated Shinbone Alley at Newcastle. Royal Ascot is a very social event and we were luncheon guests of John Brown of William Hill, which was really good. David and Dinah Nicholson, as always, invited Jo and me to their car-park buffet, as did Terry and Margaret Holdcroft, before and after racing on other days, and we went out a couple of times in the evening for a meal with some of our owners. If you notice, Jo and I are standing in front of the lost-property office. If Jo had lost her plastic card, I wouldn't have reported it stolen but would have preferred for it to remain lost!

Whilst I was at Ascot British Telecom benefited financially from all the phonecalls I made home and to various other places. One phonecall in particular was to Laura Way, apprentice Paul Bradley's agent. Reading my *Racing Post*, I noticed that after Paul was to have ridden George (Selhurstpark Flyer) in the Wokingham at 3.45, Laura had booked him to ride in the 6.30 at Newmarket. I told her to get him off the horse as on a Friday night he would be lucky to get off the M25 by 6.30, let alone be at Newmarket.

I also reminded her of our star apprentice's navigational exploits, recalling one particular incident from last year, when he was driving my car from our local meeting at Chester. I dozed off, only to be woken up by the sound of something rattling. Brad, with the car window rolled down, was throwing coins into the metal cash-point at the Mersey-effing-Tunnel, taking us near on fifty miles and a good hour out of our way. The only way Master P. Bradley could have ridden Silver Secret for his trainer S. Gollings would have been if Captain Scott of the *Starship Enterprise* had beamed him up!

In Ascot's owners' and trainers' bar, a few of us were talking about Graham Bradley (Graham was the last of the five jockeys who had been accused of cheating and then cleared of all charges) and the harm done to racing by these unfounded allegations. One of our group pointed out that inevitably punters will say there is no smoke without fire and the jockeys will now be remembered for being arrested rather than for the winners they have ridden. The racing-security official responsible certainly had something to answer for. Someone else said that the official was a character. Geoff Lewis, who always has a quip ready, said, 'Well,

JB and Jo at Royal Ascot

you're right about one thing. His name begins with a c but the second letter is not an h!'

At the end of July, on our way to Doncaster's Sunday meeting in the pouring rain, Jo and I got off to a poor start when I spotted a lone magpie on the M6 motorway; its dreaded solitary state prompted my recital, '10,9,8,7,6,5,4,3,2,1 – bad luck on your tail, sir.' We then ran into torrential rain on the M62 and were held up for a while by two separate minor road accidents. As a result, I was half an hour late for my booking as the celebrity tipster for a firm who were entertaining around fifty guests in the Lincoln Conservatory at 1.00 p.m., but I did manage to find them a few winners.

Jo and Colin, one of our travelling head-lads, saddled up Laurel Prince, our runner in the first race, the Euro-American Amateur Invitation race. When I had finished my little job, I went down to the paddock to give instructions to our French lady rider, Miss T. Botond, who lives and rides in America. As we were standing in the paddock, I felt a heavy thud in my back and my binoculars went flying. A horse dashed by out of control, with the Welshpool trainer David Evans swinging off the lead rein and the Swedish rider Mr Y. von Ballmoss hanging on for dear life. My back hurt so much, I felt like lying down, but I didn't dare. All those punters who saw it and were amazed I was still standing, would have thought instead, what a soft prat!

Next thing I heard was a voice over the Tannoy saying that Laurel Prince had bolted to the start. This I could not believe, as usually Laurel Prince would not pull a hen off the nest! Looking through my Zeiss binoculars, sure enough, our charge was flat out, three quarters of the way down to the mile straight, and as I watched, to my horror, Miss Botond bailed out. She was doing so many somersaults, one could have mistaken her for the Russian gymnast, Olga Korbut. Mercifully, she was not hurt, nor was the horse – just a bit distressed and he had to be withdrawn. I felt sorry for the rider, who on her return to the paddock was in tears and so embarrassed, but I could have laughed when she told me that from the feeling Laurel Prince gave her going to the start he would have done well in the race.

At Pontefract races the next day, Jo and I had a luncheon invitation from the Robert Bowett Motor Group, who sell Saab cars. John Morgan and I were given the job of running through the races for the forty or so guests. Between us, we picked a few winners, including my nap of the day, Gem of Wisdom in the 4.30 at Southwell, which duly obliged at 11–4. David and Trish Brown went back home with Jo to stay the night, on their way to the wake of Ken Oliver. Meanwhile, I went to Wakefield to visit my old mate Paddy Farrell in Pinderfields Hospital. The Browns and the Berrys met up later on at the Crofter's Restaurant for a slap-up meal, during which we ironed out all racing's problems.

At 11.30 a.m. on Tuesday, 29 June, the tiny parish church near Hawick probably had more people inside it than it had had for a long time, maybe more than ever before, for the celebration of the life of Kenneth Oliver, the Benign Bishop, 1 February 1914–17 June 1999. The service was devised and the hymns specially chosen by Ken, and we were told in no uncertain terms: No black ties and no tears, it's a party! As most people who knew Ken in his prime understood, Ken was a party animal. And, sure enough, a party there was, in a huge marquee up at the yard, attended by horsemen and horsewomen from all over Britain and Ireland.

Ken Oliver had the distinction of training more winners than any other trainer in Scotland. It would have been fitting if Oliberi, owned by Ken and my missus, had won the 4.15 at Hamilton, instead of finishing second, but there is no doubt that if Ken had been looking on, he would have been well pleased; with all the horses' the Olivers and the Berrys have had together over the years, there has never once been the slightest bit of moaning on either side. 'It's fun!' Ken would say, and with Ken it was fun.

On 11 May 1991, we had two runners in the Irthing Selling Race for two-year-olds at Carlisle, the 15–8 favourite Touch of Blue and Down The Middle, 20–1, owned by Jo and Ken, ridden by David Nicholls. Down The Middle had one previous run at Beverley, where he turned in a stinker.

In the paddock Ken said, 'Can I tell my pals to have their fiver on Down The Middle, Jack?'

'Touch of Blue should win,' I said. 'The way your fellow ran at Beverley was awful. In fact, if Down The Middle doesn't shape up better today, we should seriously consider sending him "down the road".'

Sod's law, Touch of Blue finished fifth and Down The Middle won, earning £2,679, which is actually more than you get for winning a similar race today, some eight years later, which shows the state of prize-money at the bottom end. The horse was put up for auction and we bought him back for three thousand two hundred guineas. Ken loved it, and he got some mileage out of that story, as he told it lots of times.

The last day in June saw Chris Deuters, our main owner, elected to the council of the Racehorse Owners' Association, heading the list of newcomers with two hundred and eighty votes. Chris is a knowledge-able and very fair man with a strong character. The ROA will benefit greatly by his presence, that I can assure you.

My old mate David Brown, who used to play cricket for Warwickshire and England, annually invites Jo and me to watch England play at Edgbaston, scheduled this year for Sunday, 4 July. Needless to say, we were looking forward to it very much as during the season we don't have time for such luxuries very often. In fact, on some Sundays, it's as hard to get out of the yard as it would be to get out of Alcatraz. This year, as you probably know, England beat New Zealand by seven wickets on the Saturday, which meant there was no play on the Sunday.

The previous day, while we were having our lunch as guests of Letherby and Christopher, one of the day's sponsors at Haydock, Derek Thomson gave a run down of all six races. It's a good thing Derek has other jobs, or he would starve to death! He sounds so convincing when he gives his selections, with the likes of 'this will win', 'this a certainty', and 'this cannot get beat'. One man at our table got out a wad that was big enough to choke a donkey and was ready to wade in until I gently warned him that Derek's tips are not always that good, as I know him of old! On our table we shared a placepot, and we were still in with a chance until the last, six- runner, race of the day, where we needed any one of our selected three horses to be placed. Unfortunately it didn't happen. We chose the last three finishers, but we certainly had a great day.

As there was no cricket on Sunday, Messrs Brown and Deuters, along with a few more, got together at the Brown residence at Furnace Mill Stud to eat the delicious food they had prepared for the cricket buffet. Chris, who is a real connoisseur of fine wines (and, as you can see from the photos, so is Jo) brought along twelve bottles of 1982 Château La Lagune, which was absolutely lovely. While we were there, we had a good look at Bolshoi, who is well on the road to recovery and we hope will be back in training with us next season.

Jo and I stayed overnight at Chris and Antonia's and the next day watched our two runners both finish second at Bath before going on to the evening meeting at Windsor, where our only runner, La Caprice, came fourth.

Six-year-old Albert the Bear, who is having a new lease of life, won his eighth race on his fiftieth start at Pontefract today, Monday, 6 July. Two years ago we bought a goat for a horse called Only For Gold, who was a bit of a worrier. The horse took an incredible dislike to the goat (whom our girls christened Hamish), so much so that if the RSPCA had looked over Only For Gold's door, they would have run us in. When we rescued Hamish we put him in with Albert, who thought he was great. If Hamish ever strayed out of Albert's sight, the horse threw a wobbler and

Jo and Chris Deuters taking turns to drink from the cup

repeatedly shouted after him. On occasions that goat got out of his box and followed Albert round the roads for an hour upsides. They were inseparable. Albert was head over heals in love with Hamish but he never looked like winning a race. Winning was the last thing on Albert's mind.

When our horses run, whoever attends the meeting has to fill in a report. In my report for Chester on 2 June, I had written:

Albert the Bear 0–95 8.8 Class C
(Drawn 8. J. Carroll. Soft going. 7 furlongs)
Jumped out well. Chases along to hold second and third position. Weakened halfway up the straight to finish fifth, beaten sixteen and a half lengths. He blew quite a bit, which would suggest he needs stronger handling at home as he must be skiving in his work. Get rid of the goat. Albert has got himself too comfortable and to boot he didn't try very hard either. Put blinkers or a visor on him. Come back a furlong and I am convinced he will be a different horse.

The next time he ran was at Carlisle on 10 June, in blinkers; he finished fourth of nineteen, from a bad draw. Albert's next run was on 23 June, when he won by two lengths. Today he has won the ten-thousand-pound feature race at Pontefract. Albert and Hamish remind me of two cows having a chat in a field. One said to the other, 'What do you think of that Mad Cow Disease?' 'I don't know. It doesn't bother me – I'm a duck!!'

13

I Thought My Numbers Were Up

On Thursday, 8 July, instead of going racing – we had runners at Southwell and Lingfield, producing a winner and two seconds – we headed, for a change, to Sheikh Mohammed's Dalham Hall Stud at Newmarket.

Jo and I, along with another thousand or so, had been cordially invited to view their stallions and have lunch. It was absolutely brilliant in one day to see such great horses as Wolfhound, Lion Cavern, Machiavellian, Pennekamp, In The Wings, Polish Precedent, Halling, Mark Of Esteem, Singspiel and the old fellow Mtoto, who were all paraded and looked superb.

It's always good when horsey people get together – you can be sure of a good laugh. At the Darley stallion parade lunch, Dick O'Gorman, David and Trish Brown, bloodstock agent Cormac McCormac, The Bride and I were talking about stallions. Cormac told us about a sale where he had been looking at yearlings for Geoff Lewis. He picked out a very nice yearling and got on the phone to give Geoff the SP on it. 'He is a lovely yearling, Geoff, with real good bone, plenty of heart-room, nice limbs and a straight mover.' Geoff, who stutters a bit, especially when he gets at all excited, said, 'Sounds good to me, C–C–Cormac. What c–c–colour is he?' 'Chestnut,' says Cormac, 'the only thing I can find wrong with him is that he has got little balls.' 'L–l–little balls,' Geoff said, 'I've got l–l–little balls, and I won the Derby!'

Today I sold our oldest horse-box to David Bridgewater. It's all plastered up with the 'Joseph Heler Cheese' logo and our name, which I hope David will paint over. A few years ago, I sold a box to Bob Gardiner, a local horse-dealer, which had our name emblazoned on the side. Shortly after a woman rang me up, gave me a real scalding and wouldn't let me get a word in edgeways, telling me our driver had far too many ponies in the box. She had seen him turning them out into a field, they looked in poor nick and I should be ashamed of myself. No wonder we didn't have many winners and she had a good mind to report me to the RSPCA. When I finally got through to her that I had sold the box, she said, 'I don't believe you. You should have repainted it before you sold it!'

The following day at Chester, the 7.00 p.m. race was a seven-and-a-half furlong apprentice race with seventeen runners. Two budding jockeys got spare rides and two horses couldn't run because their riders didn't turn up. Fellow trainer Allan Bailey was told his rider, R. Mullen, was struggling in the traffic and there was a strong possibility that he wouldn't make it to the course in time to ride. Allan said that Master Mullen had set off from Newmarket at 1.30 p.m., but who was to know he rode a bike? As there were no kids to ride the spare horses, Allan asked the weighing-room doorman, 'Is Gypsy [Alan McKay] in there? He can ride like a claimer.'

The next day at Chester we ran Ace of Parkes in the Listed race and Ninety Degrees in the two-year-old maiden, the latter owned by the Right-Angle Club, consisting of Sir Alex Ferguson, Peter Morgan and friends. Chester is Alex's local course and his presence ensured that the opening price of 8–1 shortened to 9–2 third favourite by post time. The horse finished second, beaten by just a neck, and looked all over the winner when he took up the running one and a half furlongs out; he was only collared by Coco de Mer, trained by Alan Jarvis, in the last couple of strides. On the other hand, the winning post came a stride too soon for Singsong at York in the nursery, as he was flying at the finish, to go down by a head to Fez, whose petrol had clearly run out and who was just running on fumes. As statistics go, we have trained forty-eight winners to date and would you believe fifty-eight seconds. Never before can I remember having more seconds than winners.

Much worse was to come. John Spouse, Clive Brittain's head-man (if you remember, John was the first person we employed), came with his wife, son and daughter to stay the night before Alex Ferguson's testimonial day at Haydock on Sunday. We were having a drink, reminiscing about old times, when we heard horses trotting past the house. As the hostel and all the bungalows are on the complex, nearly all our staff heard the horses and were out in force. Eight horses and one pony, loose in a paddock, had been rubbing or had run into the gate and burst it open. It was a very hot and humid night, which may have made the horses uncomfortable and restless in the first place. Alan got out the quad bike and Helen got into her car while I drove Jo's to go in search of them.

As the two cars were going down our lane, the horses turned round and came charging back towards us. One went over the top of Helen's car, giving her the fright of her life. It smashed the bonnet, windscreen and sun-roof, making a right mess of the car. I stopped, with my headlights full-on, as they were going much too fast to stop or give me a chance to get out of the way. It was impossible to ditch the cars on account of the high hedges. The horses galloped over or squeezed past the sides of the car (which was only six weeks old), doing untold damage to themselves. I can tell you, hearing the noise of horses' hooves banging on the bonnet and the top of the car was an awful experience that I wouldn't wish on anyone. When the windscreen went through, I thought my numbers were up – and I don't mean the lottery ones either. The cars were both complete write-offs.

The chase ended when we finally rounded up the horses in our cantering ring and then we led them all into our indoor school to examine them properly. The state the poor buggers was in was sickening. I thought we had a bad day when we lost Martel, but this time Peter Acton, our vet, had to put down three fillies, Crackling Rose, owned by Willie Burns, and a lovely Common Grounds filly (out of Sports Post Lady) and My Bold Girl, both owned by the firm. It was awful. By the time the vet had patched up two others and we had got the three fillies away, it was 3.30 a.m.

Hoping the day would get better, we headed for Haydock where we were running Jack Hanson and Alex Ferguson's Shinbone Alley at Haydock's testimonial raceday for Alex and we were invited to lunch on the manager's table. The race turned out to be a carbon copy of yesterday's Chester race with Ninety Degrees. Shinbone Alley was the 7–4 favourite and seemed to have the race sewn up, until he hung back

Jo's Saab

so badly half a furlong from home, probably on account of the firm going, that Barry Hills's Trouble Mountain passed him in the dying strides to win by half a length. No good blaming bad luck too much with Alex, though. He is a realist if ever there was one. He once told me he bought Andy Harrow, for what in those days was a lot of money, while he was at Aberdeen. Time after time, the ball hit the woodwork but seldom went in the net. One Saturday, after the game, people were saying what an unlucky player Andy was. Alex said, 'You're right there. He is an unlucky player. I will sell him on Monday.' And he did!

Our team set off this morning for Brighton, carrying Monday's runners, but the cab in the horse-box caught fire near Warwick. Thankfully the horses were all right. After the fire-brigade had declared it safe, the box was towed to the racecourse stables, to give the horses some rest until another of our boxes arrived to continue the journey to Brighton. When our team finally got going, they were well caught up in the Silverstone traffic, and our box didn't arrive at Brighton stables until 10.10 p.m. Roll on tomorrow!

On the 13 July, before Beverley races, Marie Matthews, the owner and breeder of our two-year-old Gem of Wisdom, the winner of his last two races, held a lunch for a few of her friends at Walkington Manor Hotel, near the racecourse, to which she kindly invited Jo and me. The hotel was the old home of ex-trainer Pat Taylor, for whom Jo was working when I first met her all those years ago. As you can imagine, the experience brought back many memories for her.

Our fine run of seconds continued at Catterick the following day with Tuscan Dream and Archie, both favourites. Archie didn't want to win. He shot clear a furlong out, then shortened up to wait for the others to catch him up. It was amusing in the Tote credit office, when I popped in to see the betting. Commentator John Hunt said, 'The handlers are just loading Quiz Master into Trap 6.' We may as well have been at the dogs, as there were some shady characters running in that six-furlong seller.

The following day, Thursday, our Francport ran second in the feature race at Bath. In the next race, the five-furlong claimer, Angie Baby, who is owned by our Sam and Charlie Williams, a pal of Sam's, also wheelchair-bound, whom he met in Tenerife, along with a couple more of their mates, ran with a ten-thousand-pound claim on her. She started 2–1 favourite even though she was drawn sixteen of eighteen, which is a near impossible task at Bath. It was no surprise that she finished only eighth but that did not deter Epsom trainer Roger Ingram from putting in a successful claim.

14

The Shirt Off My Back

Friday, 16 July was Red-Shirt Night at Pontefract, for the seventh successive year. The races were kindly sponsored by Joseph Heler, Chris and Antonia Deuters, Countrywide Freight Ltd and Weatherbys Group Ltd and produced a record turnout of sixty-five runners for our night. Pontefract's Clerk of the Course, Norman Gundill, very generously gave our Injured Jockeys Holiday Fund thirty pounds per runner and all the race sponsors' contributions also came our way. The evening is really good fun, with many of the men donning red shirts to get into the spirit of the thing, while lots of the ladies dress in red. Nearly ten thousand paying customers turned up to see six very competitive races.

Our three runners, Corunna, Antonia's Double and Albert The Bear finished third, second and third respectively, giving them all a pay-day. There is nothing worse than a horse finishing fourth and not getting paid for it. Personally, I think all fourth positions in every race should get something, and in races of ten thousand pounds or more, horses should be paid down to sixth place. Yorkshire trainer David 'Dandy' Nicholls was man of the match, scoring a double with Atlantic Viking and The Thruster. Dandy's horses always look so big and well. All credit to David, his jockey wife Alex and his team. Their horses are running out of their skins.

Jill Campion, one of our owners, and her friend Jackie Maddison sold raffle tickets for our cause. Northern Racing PRO,Graham Orange, conducted the auction which was held in the winner's enclosure. A lot of very kind people worked really hard for the night to be a success. The Tenerife beneficiaries are grateful to them all, and on their behalf, I say a big thank you.

The following Monday, I visited Paddy Farrell in hospital on the way to Beverley's evening stint. Mary, his wife, was there and I was stirring it a bit when, never having seen Paddy's hair so long, I said, 'He wants his mane pulling, Mary.' When we all worked together at Charlie Hall's in the 1950s, Mary chased Paddy off to the barber's just about every week. It's a pity there was no equality for women in the late 1950s, when I was in the army, as Mary would have made a good NCO. When I went to Oswestry for our initial training, there was a lance bombadier, a right berk called Smith, who would stand behind you when he was inspecting and shout in your ear, 'Am I hurting you, Gunner Berry?'

'No, bombadier,' I would say.

'Well, I should be, I'm stood on your bloody hair,' he would yell, even if we had only just had our hair cut a few days beforehand. That goon would have said Duncan Goodhew needed a haircut.

When I had my hair cut last week, the lady hairdresser asked, 'How many times a year do you have your hair cut?' 'Three or four,' was my reply. When she held up a mirror for me to see the back and sides, I said, 'It looks a bit sharp. You've cut a lot off.' To which she replied, 'If that's the case, you might get away with only coming back two or three times next year.'

Tuesday, 20 July 1999, was a memorable day, marking my first ever trip to Yarmouth – the last of the British Flat tracks for me to visit. It marked an even greater occasion for Sir Alex Ferguson, as it was the day he was invested with his knighthood. Sir Alex co-owns Ninety Degrees and it runs in the name of the Right-Angle Club. The horse ran at Yarmouth that very day, which, for all the football manager's fame, had to be one of the most important days in his life.

Alex can hardly have got out of the palace before he was on to me from the Savoy, ringing me up on the course at Yarmouth to have a chat about Ninety Degrees. Alex, as you would expect, was in cracking form and absolutely over the moon with the honour he had just received from the Queen.

As the horses cantered down to the start of the race, Derek Thomson, the day's commentator, reminded the large crowd that Ninety Degrees was owned in partnership with Alex Ferguson, who had just been knighted at Buckingham Palace. Derek also told the punters that it was the very first time that I had visited Yarmouth racecourse, which was a five-hundred-and-ninety-eight-mile round trip. To add more icing to Sir Alex's cake, Ninety Degrees, ridden by Richard Hughes, won the race, the fifth on the card, at odds of 6–4 – the first winning favourite of the afternoon. The combination of being a winning favourite and one owned by Sir Alex on the day of his investiture made Ninety Degrees a very popular horse and the large crowd showed their appreciation.

The next day saw yours truly at Catterick, where thirty-seven years ago that five-time champion jockey Willie Carson rode his first winner on a horse called Pinkers's Pond. To commemorate the occasion, Catterick annually stages a race, the Willie Carson/Pinker's Pond Apprentice Handicap, for apprentices who have never ridden a winner. Sycamore Lodge, ridden by nineteen-year-old Oliver Kozak, who stands five feet eleven inches tall, beat our Lunch Party by a neck. Oliver looked more like a window cleaner who had no need of ladders than a jockey, but, incredibly, he tips the scales at 8 stone 6 pounds. The scene was quite comical when the young jockey went to receive his prize from Willie, who looked half his size.

The Cockerham Recreation Committee held their third annual sportsmen's dinner at the Crofter's Hotel, near Garstang, on the evening of 23 July, which Nev, Flash and I attended. The compère, Mike King, whom I know well as he presides over lots of functions in Lancashire, is an absolute scream. Mike tells some of the simplest yet silliest jokes. He said he went into a Muslim strip club and all the men were shouting, 'Get 'em off. Show us your face!' Another one was about the time a man came up to him and said, 'I was in your class at school. Don't you remember me?' 'No, I don't,' Mike replied. 'There was no one in our class with a bald head and no teeth.'

As you can imagine, Mike took the juice out of me whenever he got the chance. The money raised went towards providing our village with new sports facilities and an extension to the hall. At the auction, I bought a framed, signed photo of Manchester United ace Ryan Giggs for a hundred and ten pounds, which I needed like a hole in the head.

Butter would not melt in their mouths

We have so many paintings and photos in our house, it looks like an art gallery.

On Saturday, we had another two seconds but I couldn't grumble really as we also had an across-the-board treble with Antonia's Double at Newcastle, Oliberi at Redcar and Lamborgini Loz who won at Lingfield.

The following Tuesday, on the way to Glorious Goodwood, I had an amusing phonecall from a gentlemen living in Newmarket. His firm was doing a promotional project and he rang to ask where I bought my red shirts, as he wanted about thirty to kit his staff out. Someone told him that I was the man to ask, as I wore red shirts all the time. The next phonecall was from home to say the local gamekeeper had just brought three of our Jack Russells, Ollie, Dave and Garry, back to the yard. He was raging because they had killed ninety per cent of his young pheasants. Looking at them, you would think butter would not melt in their mouths.

On 28 July, Crimbourne Stud, owned by Sir Eric Parker, held an open day. As Antonia and Chris were going there before racing at Goodwood, and given the fact that Miss Rossi, the mother of those two very pacy sprinters Dancing Music and Rosselli, both of which we trained, was resident, Jo and I tagged along.

It isn't easy for these studs to keep ahead of the game. Competition at the yearling sales is fierce and owning broodmares has never been an easy way to make money. In fact, I remember an old horseman who once said, 'If you want to do your worst enemy a bad turn, give him a broodmare.' However, Sir Eric did not miss a trick. You could say that he milked the cow on all four tits; he was up there with the mike giving all the spiel and doing a good job. The morning was interesting and very enjoyable. I would have liked to own one particular yearling filly, by Saddlers Wells out of Holton Gardens, who is entered for the Houghton Sales, Newmarket's premier auction, where I am certain she will make a fortune.

Usually, we do well with our Goodwood runners. Unfortunately, this year we drew a blank and had to settle for just a couple of places, although we had a most enjoyable time.

It's hard to wind down and step off the treadmill quietly when all past thoughts have been on work, but on Friday morning, for the first time in my life, at sixty-one years of age, I had a nine-hole game of golf. My partner was Janette Heler, whose other half and John Forsyth were the opposition. Call it beginner's luck if you like, but Janette and I scooped the ten-pound prize-money on offer. Although golf has never been my scene, a few of my shots were quite good. Janette and Joe said I was a natural. Personally, the only things I have found that come naturally to me are eating and drinking. Afterwards we had a great lunch as guests of Chris and Antonia in their box.

August 1, our open day, started in brilliant sunshine. Unfortunately, it took place the same day as the Royal Lancashire Show, twenty-six miles away, which lost us many locals. Even so, around two thousand people attended. Everyone seemed to enjoy themselves, the kids loved Fred the Red, the Manchester United mascot that Lynn, Alex Ferguson's secretary, kindly arranged for us. It was also fantastic to see the

Lunch at Goodwood

carthorse trot. Bob Gardner provided six magnificent shire horses. One, named Valiant, is one of the biggest shires in the world, standing a massive 19.2 hands high. Three jump jockeys rode against three Flat jockeys on our middle grass gallop. The winner was National Hunt jockey Brian Storey. I got on the back of the second, behind Roddy Lappin. You might say we had too much weight or we would have won. Maybe Brian is used to riding this kind of horse.

Unfortunately Sharron's parachute jump, the highlight of the day, couldn't take place on account of a thunderstorm at the airstrip. Sharron who had waited for hours for the off, dressed up like Biggles, was gutted. She had looked forward so much to doing the jump and had even previewed the event on the previous day's Morning Line. If nothing else, she seems to like living dangerously. Sharron won't let her many sponsors down and will now do the tandem jump with Danny Smith on the 21 August, or, failing that, she may try her hand at swimming across a shark-infested pond! All in all, the day was great. We had a lot of fun and raised £12,262 for the fund, with more to come.

The Racing Channel team filmed the day's events, which included yours truly being interviewed by Gordon Brown without a red shirt on, as Adrian Ross, the DJ, had previously auctioned it off for sixty-five pounds. Chris Deuters matched that figure for another of my shirts. So if you see Flat jockey Gypsy McKay in a red shirt that is far too big for him, you know where he got it from. Or if you see a certain ROA council member bursting out of a red shirt, it could be one of my cast-offs.

For the past few years, John and Gail Stephenson have run an all-bottles-of-alcohol tombola stall and donate the takings to our IJHF and local charities. This year the beneficiaries were SS John Fisher and Thomas More High School and John's local church, the Holy Saviour, in Nelson.

Michael Hutchinson, a director of Ripon racecourse, generously invited The Bride and myself to a lunch celebrating the course's centenary year for the Ripon Race Company Ltd, although the city of Ripon has enjoyed an active role in the Sport of Kings for more than three hundred years. At lunch, I was drawn next to Mr Wilmott Smith, a lovely old man who was an owner with the late Beverley trainer, Snowy Gray, for whom I had the odd ride years ago. We were talking about yesterday's open day and he kindly said what a useful salesman I must be, to sell all the raffle tickets we did. This sent a shudder down my spine as I thought that I would need to be a good salesman with the yearling sales about to start in a month's time. (I have been known to buy quite a few yearlings before I have found owners for them!)

As we were leaving Ripon, Peter Amory, who plays Chris Tate in the TV series *Emmerdale Farm*, gave me a twenty-pound note for the holiday fund, which had been given to him by a lady in return for a kiss and a promise that the note went to charity. I give Claire, Peter's real-life missus, a kiss every time I see her, as we have been friendly for years, and she doesn't charge me a penny!

The Racing Channel showed a film of our open day after racing on Tuesday. It started with Gordon Brown, their presenter, coming through the stalls at the entrance to our yard to the dulcet tones of 'The Jolly Farmer' being sung by yours truly in the background. Recently I was talking to Danish female jockey Le Tolboll, a good friend of ours. Le told

123

me that at Klampenbag, Denmark's premier track where they run their Derby, the jockeys all have a signature song which is played when they enter the winner's enclosure having come first. Most jockeys choose fashionable tracks from the likes of Boyzone or the Spice Girls. Le's chosen song is 'The Jolly Farmer'. The racegoers all cracked up to start with when they heard the cattle mooing and the chickens cackling, but now they all love it.

On Wednesday, after Pontefract races, thinking what a waste of time it was going there after watching our two-year-old beat just one in the maiden and Miss Grapette finish third in the claimer, I popped in again to Pinderfields Hospital to see my old mate Paddy Farrell, who, after nine weeks, is still in there on account of bed sores. It was a hot and humid evening, with not a breath of air about. Paddy and some other patients in the ward have to be turned every couple of hours. Some had so little movement that they would not have been able to swat a fly that landed on their nose.

Glancing round that hospital ward, you could see what dire hands had been dealt to some of the inmates. Paddy himself had fallen out of bed, suffered with his kidneys, had trouble with an elbow and a bout of uncontrollable spasms, not to mention a bloodshot eye and a dose of diarrhoea. On top of that Heinz of mishaps, the next day Paddy was going to have a tube put down his throat, with a camera fitted to enable the doctor to see his insides.

Mary, Paddy's wife, had been to see him beforehand. Being the diplomat that she is, Mary tried to break the bad news gently, reminding him that the roof at home had been leaking so badly that a part of it would have to be replaced, and that, for good measure, the water had completely ruined the carpet. Perhaps she did not want the old jockey feeling too sorry for himself.

Trainer Bryan McMahon, a long-time pal of mine, recently had a heart attack. On a scale of one to ten, he had an eight, which is quite serious. Joy, his wife, said Bryan needed to be kept quiet and have lots of rest. I sent my old mate a get-well card. According to Joy, when Bryan opened it he almost had another attack, he was laughing that much.

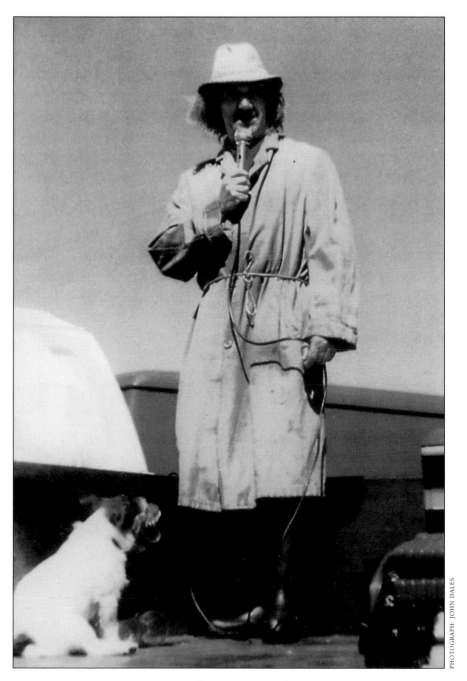

PHOTOGRAPH: JOHN DALES

JB sings 'The Jolly Farmer' on the open day

GREETINGS CARD ©PAPERLINK LTD and MARTIN BROWN

The get-well card for Bryan
McMahon from JB

Get well soon, mate.
Jack

On Monday, 9 August, I again donned my black tie to attend the Preston crematorium for Gladys's funeral. For the past few weeks she has been living in an old people's home, as she became increasingly unable to cope following her fall in February. Really one shouldn't feel too sorry for her, as she had a good innings, reaching the ripe old age of eighty-four. Gladys and Bob were very much in love all their lives. I am amazed that she lasted as long as she did without him, as she missed him terribly. If there is such a thing as heaven, I hope that they will be together again now.

On a lighter note, Bob and Gladys loved a bit of fun and a joke, and they wouldn't want me to be morbid. One day Gladys and her grandson were going for a stroll. Outside the graveyard was a stone propped up against the wall. 'It looks as if those hooligans have thrown that headstone over the wall. They've got no respect, the young people today. Eighty-four, the same age as me,' said Gladys. Then, as the letters were smaller than the figures, 'Bend down and see who it was and where he came from.'

'It says "miles from Newcastle",' said the boy.

On the same day, before I left for Thirsk evening races, bloodstock-agent Sam Bullard, a good friend of trainer Mikey Heaton-Ellis, rang to tell me that Mikey had passed away. Most considerately, Sam wanted to make sure that I knew before reading about it in the *Racing Post* the next day.

All winners are nice, be it a seller or a group race, but I must confess that when Richard Hughes rode our twelve-year-old Amron (Ronnie) to victory over seven rivals in the ten-furlong race a Ayr, it was particularly sweet. Ronnie was trying this trip for the first time and, starting at a generous 20–1, went from last to first, to beat the favourite, Bowclifffe, by one and a half lengths. This was Ronnie's second win of the season and his sixteenth in all from a hundred and nine starts. The old boy has so many admirers and several of our owners rang to say how pleased they were, knowing him as they do. No sooner had the old boy passed the post than Robert Ward, a punter who had watched the race from the William Hill betting shop in Knightsbridge, rang our yard to congratulate us. He was just so chuffed even though he hadn't had a shilling on the old horse.

127

Friday 13 is not a good day for the superstitious, but it wasn't so bad for our victorious two-year-olds, Glenrock and Susie's Flyer. Ridden by Seb Sanders, both duly obliged at Lingfield. The Surrey track is a very lucky one for our yard. At the time of writing, twenty of the fifty-three two-year-olds that we have run there have won. Unfortunately, I wasn't at Lingfield to see our winners. I did the evening stint at Catterick and watched Palacegate Jack just hack round, not doing a tap, in the rain. However, I was invited to fellow trainer Denys Smith's seventy-first-birthday party at the course, which was very nice.

Leeds United played Manchester United at Old Trafford the next day. Steve Allan, an owner with trainer David Evans, knows I am a Leeds United fan and had invited me to his box to watch the game and to have a meal after the match before going on to Haydock's evening meeting, where we were running the Right-Angle Club's horse, Ninety Degrees. The kick-off was at twelve noon, and with the ground being just under an hour's drive away, I had time to work most of the horses before I left. It was a great match – although Manchester United beat Leeds 2–0. I did manage to win a few bob, as I had a small investment on Dwight Yorke to score the first goal. Just as I had left the ground, Alex, who was also going to Haydock Park to see his horse run, rang my mobile to tell me that he had heard that the meeting had been cancelled due to water-logging.

At Ripon, we ran Ansellman (Marco) and Bon Ami in the course's richest race, the William Hill Great St Wilfred. Bon Ami, ridden by the under-used Alex Greaves, finished second, beaten a short-head by Tim Easterby's Pipalong. The narrow defeat proved quite expensive as the winner picked up a cool £24,125 and our man collected £7,250. I am not complaining, as my turn came at our village fête where I had entered a photo in the 'funniest snap with caption' section. It was of a bunch of our horses from the rear, working on our all-weather gallop, and was entitled 'Heads Down – Bottoms Up', and it won!

Last year I was pressurised into baking a fruit-cake. To be honest, I hadn't a clue how to make a cake. Jo stood me upsides our kitchen table and made one to show me how to do it. The cake looked real good, but it did not finish in the frame in the show. Bob Stevens from Bumbles

Heads Down – Bottoms Up

restaurant looked after the cake in the show for me (not as if it was going anywhere) and the next night a few of us went to Bumbles for a meal and found that for a giggle Bob had written on his board:

TODAY'S SPECIAL
JACK BERRY'S FRUIT CAKE
£2.50p PER SLICE

Alex Ferguson had a slice and he said it was all right, and he's never looked back since. In fact, he has even got himself knighted!

15

The Best Jump For Ten Years

On Monday, 16 August, we had a visit from the Jockey Club vet, Keith Mason, along with two veterinary technicians, to take samples from the horses; in February 1998 a programme of random testing for horses in training was introduced and today was our turn. It didn't disrupt our day, as on Mondays the horses do roadwork. The only horses to canter are the runners up to Wednesday or the fat and lazy ones. Keith got the horses' passports from our office staff and the lads brought him out the horses he wanted to test.

I couldn't hang around for too long as, a couple of weeks ago, I became a trustee of the Injured Jockeys Fund. Today was my first meeting, which was held in the stewards' room at York racecourse, a room I can proudly say that in thirty years with a licence I have never before been in. Other trustees in attendance were Lord Oaksey, Brough Scott, Dick Saunders, John Smith, Peter Scudamore, John Fairley and Simon McNeill. The meeting started just after 1.00 p.m. and carried on, non-stop, until just before 5.00 p.m.

One cannot fail to be amazed at the dedication of the chairman, chief executive, the almoners and the trustees. The workload they get through needs to be seen to be believed. With all the help and support the Injured Jockeys Fund provides for so many people, I am honoured and privileged to have been appointed a trustee. I will try to serve it well.

Joe Heler, the owner of Ace of Parkes, doesn't mess about. His horse is way overrated in handicaps and not good enough to win stakes or conditions races. I told Joe the horse needed to come down a stone to win and said I would contact the adjuster to see how he justifies his high opinion of the horse and hopefully get the horse dropped to a winning mark. I must say that in the past my efforts to get handicappers to reduce their ratings have not met with much success. We all know handicappers have not got an easy job, but if a horse has a big weight, starts at 20–1 and finishes out the back, with the jockey chasing its head off, the horse wants the weight reducing wholesale, not by just a couple of pounds. Often, by the time some horses are let off the hook and come down in the weights, they have lost the zest for racing. Following my chat with Colin Vickers, the sprint handicapper, he reduced Ace by four pounds.

When I told Joe what the assessor had done and how Ace was getting flat and disheartened, Joe said, 'Well, let's get two stone off straight away and have him cut.' Which we did. Joe bred the horse and really likes him. In Joe's heart I think he would rather have had the vet castrate the handicapper, probably without an anaesthetic, than his horse. I must add, the way I sometimes feel about the handicapper's treatment, I would have held him for the vet while he did him!

Lancashire Radio came to the yard with their presenter, Sally Naden, on Friday, 20 August, as part of the Jim Bowen programme called *Workers' Playtime*. It was good, as it gave a light-hearted 'window' on a working place and went out live. Iona Wands had a chat with Sally on the mike as she was riding Lunch Box round the yard. I thought Iona would never stop talking. If the Racing Channel ever hear Iona, Alex Hammond will have to look out. If there were listeners who had never heard of Lunch Party before, they certainly know all about him now. Quite right too, as the kid has ridden him seven winners and she loves the old fellow to bits!

On Saturday, 21 August, the tandem parachute jump Sharron Murgatroyd couldn't do on our open day because of poor weather conditions was going ahead. Sharron, with her helping pal, Janet Boston, set off from Newmarket at 2.30 a.m. to be at the Cockerham Parachute Club for 9.00 a.m. Although we had runners at Chester and Ripon, I thought it only fair, as I had got Sharron into it, to go up in the plane with her. Keeping in touch with the club on my mobile from the yard before countdown, I was told there was not enough wind to do the jump until after one o'clock, which gave me ample time to work the horses before I left for the airfield. Colonel Eddie York, his wife Sarah,

Sharron Murgatroyd with the instructor

John and Linda O'Hara, along with Sharron's mum, sister and other relatives, turned out to witness the jump and give the lass some staunch support. Sharron, strapped to the instructor, Dave Smith, loved every minute of the event.

I was co-pilot in the plane. As Sharron and Dave jumped out, the mad thing let out a resounding 'Yeee–Hah!' That girl has got some guts! On the return journey, Kevin, the pilot, let me fly the plane almost to Blackpool, then over our yard and gallops until just before we landed. It was great. Although I was thousands of feet up in the air, there was still no escape from the yuppie phone. Jo rang to say that our two-year-old

Glenrock had just won at Chester. Good job I didn't do the jump. That would have been some sight, me on my mobile, dropping out of the sky!

When Sharron got back to base, you couldn't shut her up at any price, she was so excited.

'Did you enjoy that, mate?' I asked. 'Was it good?'

'Was it good? Was it good? That was the best jump I have had for ten years!'

Except for the Yorks, who had to go home, the rest of us went back to our house for a couple of celebration bottles of Ruinart champagne. Then on to Bumbles for soup and sandwiches to round off a great day for that brave girl to remember for the rest of her life. Fittingly, Sharron was made Lanson Lady of the Month for August. She will be presented with her champagne in the winner's enclosure at Goodwood on 10 September.

On Sunday, Norma and Roy Peebles visited the yard to see their horses Amron and Nifty Major. On hearing about Sharron's day, Norma quite innocently asked, 'When she did the jump, did she do it in her wheelchair?' If I had laughed any more, I would have cried.

I have just received official confirmation from the executors of the late Captain Tim Forster that our holiday fund has had a great boost. Apparently, the captain had watched a video of the Tenerife holiday, and thought it so worthwhile that he immediately rang up his solicitor to make the necessary arrangements.

On Wednesday, 24 August, Johnny Fenwick-Clenell, Clerk of the Course at Carlisle, very kindly staged a race in my honour: the European Breeders' Fund Jack Berry Farewell Stakes. Over the years, as both jockey and trainer, I have had some marvellous moments at Carlisle. Fifty-nine horses trained by yours truly have passed the post first. I would love to have won the Jack Berry Stakes with our runner, Red Sonny, but, Sod's Law, he ran a stinker and was last! The race was won by Jailhouse Rock, trained by Sir Mark Prescott, who always calls me Uncle Jack and for whom I have the utmost respect and admiration. Sir Mark is the best in the game at placing his horses, is very much his own man, sees to every detail and is in total control. Though he doesn't suffer fools gladly, he is a great sport and a most generous gentleman.

After the race, I presented the winning connections with their trophy, after Teddy Robinson, the course chairman, had climbed on to the podium and given a bit of spiel, presenting me with a nice pair of cut glasses. Truthfully, I love Carlisle and it's great in winter to go for a day's jumping. However, not all my memories of Carlisle are good. Many years ago, on my first day back riding following a lengthy injury, I rode there in the novice chase. Unfortunately for me, the horse dived over the first fence and fell at the second, and in the fall I broke my wrist. The horse's trainer had told me it was a good jumper. I think in those days some of the trainers must have shown their horses photographs of fences rather than have them jump them. That particular horse was a spare ride on the day, its intended jockey having gone sick or cried off. Little did I know that the trainer had asked one or two of the other jockeys to ride it before I got to the course, but they had refused knowing that the horse was a bit of a bone breaker. I never gave it a second thought when the trainer came into the weighing-room with his colours and asked me if I would ride the crab. He knew that, with me being a freelance, if I didn't have a ride in the race already, I would jump at the chance. Except for the jockeys riding in the race, you couldn't find the rest with radar. Most likely they had taken cover in the toilets, knowing full well that I would ride the bike if asked, which would save them the embarrassment of saying no and jeopardising any chance of better rides from the trainer in future.

Speedy James was a fast two-year-old last year, winning his first two starts at Newcastle and Newmarket. He then finished second to the champion filly Bint Allayl in the National Stakes at Sandown, giving her ten pounds. Unfortunately, Jimmy's form dipped afterwards. On his début this season, he ran a sound race to finish third to the useful Noble One and Flanders at Newmarket. Today, Saturday, 28 August, we ran him in a conditions race at Nottingham, where he missed the break and never got into the race. His owner, Edward St George, was disappointed with his run. As Jimmy's owner pays the piper, he has every right to call the tune and send his horses to be trained wherever he wishes. The inevitable phonecall came from Mary Lowe, Mr St

▲WITHERS

12 GOUGH SQUARE LONDON EC4A 3DW TELEPHONE +44 (0)20 7936 1000 FAX +44 (0)20 7936 2589 DX 160 LONDON/CHANCERY LANE
e-mail mailto@withers.co.uk   web site http://www.withers.co.uk

RJP/CVK/jkd

20 August 1999

Jack Berry MBE
Mosside Racing Stables
Cockerham
Nr Lancaster
LA2 0ES

Dear Mr Berry

Estate of Captain T A Forster deceased

We act on behalf of Captain Forster's executors, Sir Philip Payne-Gallwey, Mr and Mrs M Wiggin and Brian Stevens of this office in relation to the administration of his estate.

As I believe you may be aware, Captain Forster left a legacy of £25,000 to be added to the funds you raise annually for the Injured Jockeys' Fund for the purpose of sending injured jockeys on holiday.

The executors are now in a position to pay out the legacies and I therefore enclose a cheque for £25,000 in settlement. May I please trouble you to acknowledge receipt by signing and returning to me the duplicate copy of this letter.

Yours sincerely

Christopher King

Received a cheque for £25,000.

Signed...

Date.....23 August 1999.

90000/1-PCL2-130364/1

George's secretary. The horse is going to David Nicholls to be trained. At least the way Dandy's horses are running, winning just about every sprint handicap in sight, it's a good choice. When Jimmy recovers his old form and gets his act together, he is a good horse. No one likes losing good horses, but it happens.

It was the same in 1991, when our yard broke all sorts of records and appeared to be winning everything. Our hundredth winner of the season came on 17 July, when Our Fan won at Hamilton. We had the offer of dozens of horses, far more than we had room for. As the saying goes, success breeds success.

At the time of writing, we have trained sixty-three winners so far this season. You may say that's not great from past years, but there are only five trainers from about four hundred with licences in the whole country with more winners. If I grumbled at that, other trainers would think I was a greedy prat, and rightly so. Had we trained that amount of Flat winners in a season twenty years ago, I would have done backward flips. To date, with sixteen hundred and forty-seven winners on the board (at home and abroad, on the Flat and over the sticks), even if we haven't pleased everyone, I am grateful and more than satisfied with my record.

16

We Nearly Broke the World Record

Now it's getting towards time to restock with yearlings. It's always advisable to go round the studs to see as many youngsters as possible prior to the sales, especially the homebreds. After the Beverley meeting on 28 August, I visited the famous Sledmere Stud to cast my eye over a full sister to Gem of Wisdom, the winner of two races this season, who is owned and bred by Marie Matthews.

Sledmere Stud is open to the public in summer. It was once the biggest stud in England, with three hundred and twenty horses in residence. Grey Monus, winner of the 1873 Two Thousand Guineas, and Ridge Wood, winner of the 1949 St Leger, were bred there. Nowadays, Sledmere, owned by Sir Tatton Sykes, stands the stallions Factual and River Falls.

Alan visited Bearstone Stud to view their yearlings. Bearstone stand Mind Games (Dennis), his sire Puissance and Tragic Role. Dennis will have his first runners next season. Alan said they were nice sorts. Hopefully, they will do well; we owe their old man a favour, as he gave our yard its first Royal Ascot win. Jo and I went to Furnace Mill Stud the next day to look at their yearlings, many of which are destined for next week's St Leger sale.

On Monday, our two-year-old filly Consideration arrived back from the Animal Health Trust at Newmarket, following an operation to remove some floating chips from her knee. Jack Clayton, the filly's owner, was told the estimated price of the operation would be around a thousand pounds. Jack thought that was expensive enough, but when the bill arrived it was sixteen hundred and fifty – ever so slightly over the estimate. I wonder what the costs are, and who foots the bill, for the operations seen on the vets' programmes on TV, where a couple of vets, with assistants, are operating on a dog or a cat? I am told that one of our local vets charges thirty-five pounds to castrate a rabbit. If that isn't daylight robbery, I don't know what you call it. Another local friend of ours was charged £287.67 to do some tests on her pet rabbit and then put him to sleep. No wonder these rapists and child molesters get away with a few months' imprisonment. It must be too expensive to cut the prats.

Today, 3 September, instead of going to our local meeting at Haydock to see Red Typhoon win for the Red-Shirt Brigade, I went jumping to Sedgefield. My role there, along with Trevor Taylor (part-owner of Solares, the horse Sam had his fateful fall from at Sedgefield), was to present the winner's trophy, and best-turned-out prize to the winning lad, for the Sam Berry Novice Chase, the race which Sedgefield very kindly stage annually.

It looks like my last chance of training a Group 1 winner disappeared the following day at Haydock, when our Rosselli finished out the back behind Diktat, a member of the all-conquering Godolphin team. Rosselli is entered for the Group 1 Prix de L'Abbaye at Longchamp on the 3 October. Before we consider that event, he will run in the Group 3 Stillorgan Park Hotel Flying Five race in Ireland next Saturday.

At the Epsom meeting on the same day, we won the Victor Chandler Five-Furlong Dash, desperately trying to beat the course record of 53.6 seconds. A cool £50,000 was on offer from the racecourse: £25,000 to the owner, £10,000 to the trainer (that would have been nice!), £5,000 each to the stable, the jockey and the Animal Health Trust. Our runner, Tuscan Dream, is by Clantime, the horse we trained to win the Surrey Stakes at Epsom on Derby Day in 1983. Tuscan, from a favourable fourteen draw, shot out of the gate like something nasty off a shovel and was chased all the way to the line by Zaragossa and others trying to make a name for themselves in the record books. Our man won by one and a half lengths, carrying eight stone nine pounds, with Paul Bradley's five pounds claim off, to beat Dandy Nichols' Brecongill Lad. The recorded time was 53.85 seconds, just a quarter of a second off the world record, on good going. What a shame the gutsy, determined effort the little fellow put up for us didn't come off. Indigenous, trained by Dick Thrale at Epsom, and ridden by Lester Piggott, set the current world record of 53.6 seconds on 2 June 1960, on reportedly firm going. Actually the going was hard, Ron Smyth, the Epsom trainer, told me one Derby Day, when my old pal Willie Stevenson and I were having lunch at Ron's house before racing. In fact, Ron said that there were half-inch cracks in the ground, it was so dry. The time was also hand recorded, which isn't as reliable as electronic timing. Thanks to the modern watering policy, it won't be easy to break the thirty-nine-year-old record, but nothing would give the Deuters, Tuscan Dream's owners, more pleasure than to hold the world's sprinting record.

On the first day of Doncaster's St Leger Sale, 7 September, I went with every intention of not buying too many yearlings, my thinking being that it is a long yearling season and there is plenty of time. In any case, the race planners have moved the goalposts somewhat. Up to a couple of seasons ago, every racecourse was compelled to stage a two-year-old race on every card. Now clerks of the courses are encouraged not to have early two-year-old races. It is pointless having too many sharp, precocious youngsters in the yard, unless one runs two or three in the same race. That, I can tell you, is a recipe for disaster and the owners don't like it. The days of Provideo, Nagwa, Timeless Times and the like, whose wins ran into double figures in a season, have gone. If the moderate two-year-old has not won its maiden by the middle of June, it will struggle to win that year, a fact the auctioneers do not dwell on when squeezing the last guinea out of the purchasers at the sales.

However, this is a great sale, and, as usual, there were some good sorts there. The St Leger Sale always throws up lots of winners and we have bought a good many of them in the past. When Lot 53, a lovely American-bred top-line colt by Eagle Eyed out of a Bustino mare, came into the ring, Richard Milner, one of our owners and a good judge of a horse, loved him. The horse was duly knocked down to yours truly, on Richard's behalf, for ten thousand guineas. Alan and I looked at several more youngsters and between us we secured another three, including a very sharp-looking Clantime, which Alan bought for just six thousand guineas.

Jo and I always stay at the Moat House, where the leisure facilities are excellent, and after the sales we went for a quick swim and sauna. Derek

Thomson wasn't there this year, but a few years ago it was a wonder he wasn't locked up. The bold Derek came into the mixed sauna starkers. There was no water to throw on the coals. 'We need some water to get the heat up, mate,' I said. Without batting an eyelid, Derek picked up the wooden bucket and walked out of the sauna. The girls in the swimming-pool couldn't believe their eyes as Tommo smiled and greeted them with a – 'Good-morning!' The girls must have liked what they saw and thanks to the bush telegraph next morning there were twice as many of them in the pool – only the big fellow didn't turn up!

In the evening, we met up with the Browns, Deuters and Turnbulls for a first-class meal at Hamiltons, near the racecourse stables. The main topic of conversation, apart from the sales, was how unlucky Tuscan Dream was not to have rung the bell and won fifty grand at Epsom.

The next day, our sole runner, Ansellad, ran in the two-hundred-thousand-pound St Leger Yearling Sales Race. Back at the evening session of the sales, our first strike was a filly by our ex-champion sprinter, Mind Games, for thirteen thousand guineas. I was keeping my powder dry, ready to have a shot at a lovely bay colt by the first-season sire Charnwood Forest, submitted by Tommy Doherty, the man who owned our 1988 Ayr Gold Cup winner, So Careful. Chris Deuters and I tried very hard, but were the bridesmaids again, at forty-six thousand guineas. Finally, we struck oil when giving twenty thousand guineas for Lot 269, a full brother to Tuscan Dawn and Tuscan Dream, bred by Frazer Hines and his wife, Liz.

In the bar afterwards, we had a drink, which led to a bit of a singsong. International bloodstock agent Jimmy Byrnes sang his party piece, 'The Crystal Chandeliers', which was good but not good enough to warrant giving up the day job. For a giggle, I went round the bar with my lid, and collected Jimmy a few bob.

The number of our purchases rose to twelve the following night. A good-looking colt by Mukaddamah, bought on behalf of Andy Miller, was the most expensive. The following day at the races, Brian Ansell (Ansellad's owner), said to me, 'I see you were the under-bidder last night on an expensive yearling.'

'Yes,' I said, 'and what a really nice sort he was.'

'You're right,' said Brian. 'Where did you stop at?'

Not thinking, I said, 'At the Moat House. I have done for years.' Lambourn trainer Bryan Smart was listening and couldn't control himself for laughing.

Although we ran two horses in the sprints without success on Friday, we had a great day, as it was the annual get-together of the injured ex-jockeys in a marquee by the paddock. It's always good to see the likes of George Slack, Jack Dowdeswell, Johnny O'Hara, John Kenneally, Jon Haynes, Colin Teague, Paddy Broderick, Peter Dunn, Cliff Boothman, Des Cullen and so many other old friends, many of whom we never see from one year to the next.

With so much help from so many thoughtful and generous people, the target of a hundred thousand pounds was reached for the holiday fund. In fact, a cheque for £100,054 was handed over to Lord Oaksey OBE, the fund's chairman. During the afternoon, John and I had a chat about the fund's activities with Derek Thompson (with his clobber on) on Channel 4, in between races. We mentioned racehorse owner Robert Hitchens, who had very kindly donated a million pounds – yes, a million pounds – to the Injured Jockeys Fund. We are deeply grateful to him.

At their meeting at York the trustees decided, subject to Mr Hitchens' approval, that two hundred and fifty thousand pounds would go to ensuring the continuation of the annual holiday in Tenerife, which will now be called the Robert and Elizabeth Hitchens Holiday, and that the International Spinal Research Trust Fund would receive two hundred and fifty thousand pounds a year for the next three years.

At the races, I also managed to have a chat with Matthew Tester, the two-year-old handicapper, regarding his logic in raising Red Typhoon fourteen pounds, the biggest hike for any horse in the whole week's ratings, for winning a mere claimer at Haydock. The filly had previously run in two nurseries, finishing sixth of twelve at Newcastle, beaten three lengths off a rating of sixty-four. At Musselburgh, she had been beaten three and a half lengths when rated sixty-three. Mr Tester told me that he had been fair to the filly, and that he could have put her up more.

That I do believe, as handicappers have your nuts in the wringer and do as they like. If the filly could not win off a rating of sixty-three, how on earth can she win off seventy-seven? Weight will bring horses and donkeys together. It will even stop trains. Handicappers stop more horses winning races than all the jockeys and trainers put together, and don't have to account for their actions to the stewards, either. Rather than let me win a round, Mr Tester argued that Red Typhoon beat Paris Lights, rated eighty-seven, at Haydock. 'Yes,' I said, 'but we put our filly in the claimer at Haydock with a weight of eight stone two pounds to give her a chance to win. Paris Lights' trainer put his horse in the race with nine stone three!'

At Haydock, Red Typhoon, Maron and Paris Lights started 9–2 co-favourites and finished, respectively, first, third and seventh, so the punters and the bookies were not far wrong. Since finishing third at Royal Ascot in June, Paris Lights came last in his next two races. His owner and trainer must have lost faith in him even to consider entering him in a claimer, and the horse was clearly overrated at eighty-seven. A few weeks later Paris Lights was sold at Doncaster Sales for just five thousand four hundred guineas, confirming his owner's loss of faith, proving that Red Typhoon beat a load of moderate animals at Haydock and the handicapper overreacted.

More than likely, horse assessors think that most trainers are selfish prats, set on pulling strokes. But that is not the case and when we complain, we have to listen to so-called explanations which would give your backside earache, like naughty schoolboys. The bottom line is that we want to train winners and do the best for our owners and horses. It is hard enough to win races without the weightwatchers stopping us. On occasions they certainly have the right name, handi-capper! On the whole, over the years, they have been a handicap to me and we have trained far more winners in conditions races than we have in handicaps.

Trainers are not looking for favours, they just want fair dos. It would be a much fairer system if trainers could appeal to an ombudsman, such as race-reader Alan Amiss or Jim McGrath of Timeform, rather than get overrated by someone sat behind a desk pushing a pen who probably would not know a horse if it kicked him. There wouldn't be many cases won in the court if the judge was also the jury.

At Doncaster's final evening sale, Alan and I bought another two yearlings, making the grand total of fifteen heading for Cockerham. On Saturday morning, Jo took Terry Holdcroft and me to catch the plane from Leeds Airport to see Rosselli finish fifth in the Group 3 Stillorgan Park Hotel Flying Five at Leopardstown. The race was won by Tedburrow, trained here in Lancashire by Eric Alston. We had our first Group winner at Leopardstown with Bri-Eden in the Ballyhogan Stakes back in 1983. Terry and I didn't have much time in Ireland, as we had to catch the 7.00 p.m. plane back to Manchester, but we did manage a couple of glasses of Guinness at Dublin Airport, which was great. God knows what we do with the Guinness over here, but it tastes an awful lot better in Ireland. That sounds a bit Irish, so it does!

Fresh from finding owners for two of the Doncaster yearlings, on Sunday evening, Jo and I were invited by Willie Morgan to the Howard Keel NSPCC Golf Classic Gala Dinner and Cabaret at the Piccadilly Hotel in Manchester. It was absolutely brilliant. Willie is a friend of mine who played football for Manchester United and Scotland. Live on stage with Howard Keel, who still sings well despite his age, were Rick Wakeman, Johnny Mathis and the funniest man you ever did see, Norman Collier. Celebrities from all kinds of sport and showbiz were there, including Willie Thorne, Dennis Taylor, Nigel Mansell, Bill Roache, Derek Thompson, Duncan McKenzie, Howard Kendall, Jasper Carrrott, Kevin Whateley, Stan Boardman, and many more. It was three o'clock in the morning when we hit the sack, and before I knew it, it was time to be up and about the yard. Work hard, play hard!

Next Saturday is the Ayr Gold Cup. It is common knowledge that the Cup is my favourite race on my number-one course. Quite a few reporters have been in touch to remind me and ask about the chances of Bon Ami, who was short-headed by Pipalong in the Great St Wilfred recently. Janette Sykes from the *Racing Review* came to do a feature. Manchester United's radio station rang for a chat about Sir Alex Ferguson's involvement in racing. It's a secret, a surprise for Alex in his testimonial year. (I hope they tell him about it before he reads this book, as I intend to ask him if he would mind writing the foreword.)

Wednesday, 16 September, the eve of Ayr's Western Meeting, proved a bit chaotic. At about 11.00 p.m., while Jo and I were watching the film *The Horse Whisperer* on TV, the phone rang. It was the mother of one of our girls, reporting that her daughter had fallen out with her fiancé, who also works for us. The daughter had found a number left on the boyfriend's mobile phone, which she rang, only to discover that it was another bird. Just as horses have to be trained, so staff problems have got to be sorted out. I had heard the fax phone go in the office earlier so I went round to retrieve the message from the machine. It was from Mary Lowe, Edward St George's secretary, stating that her boss would like his other horse, Brave Burt, to go to Jeremy Noseda in Newmarket. Shortly after that, there was some banging and clattering in the yard. Ron Popely's two-year-old, My Boy Harry, was cast in his box, to complete the treble.

Every year Jo and I book into the sovereign suite at the Fairfield House Hotel for the Ayr Western Meeting, and will continue to do so after I have hung up my boots. We had a few runners on Thursday and Friday which all ran well without giving the judge an anxious moment, although Susie's Flyer, a two-year-old owned by Luke O'Reilly from Co. Covan, won at Newbury by four lengths.

If Matthew Tester can put up Red Typhoon by fourteen pounds for winning a crap claimer, what's he going to do with Susie, beating eight previous winners. Susie's success made her our fifteen hundreth home Flat winner. We celebrated with the Deuters over an Indian meal at the Ruype Restaurant in Ayr, and a couple of bottles back at the Fairfield Hotel.

Today is *the* day of the year, the Ayr Gold Cup. My interest in the race started when I was an apprentice at Charlie Hall's. Towser Gosden, John Gosden's father, broke the long journey from Lewes to Ayr by boarding his horses for a few days at our jumping yard at Towton. As I was light, I got to ride these fantastic Flat horses with the Gosden lads. To measure our big jumpers against these slick, sharp, fast horses would be like comparing tractors and racing cars. The Gosden lads were always talking about winning the Ayr Gold Cup, just as we would talk about the Cheltenham Gold Cup or the Grand National. This made me think that if I was ever lucky enough to train, I would dearly love to put

PHOTOGRAPH: KENNETH BRIGHT

Winning the Ayr Gold Cup in 1988 with So Careful

my name on that Ayr Gold Cup. The dream came true when we won in 1988 with So Careful (Albert).

Everyone, especially everyone in the North, wants to win the Ayr Gold Cup and every year lots of horses get balloted out of the great race. Dave McHarg, the then Clerk of the Course at Ayr, Mike Dillon of Ladbroke's and I talked all night at the Caledonian Hotel over a few drinks and invented the overflow race, the Silver Cup of today. We even went further and said that the race is so popular, there should be a third division, called the Bronze Cup or the Tin Cup.

Bon Ami ran in the Great Race. It would have been a big thrill to have won the race for my long-time friend, Ken Ivory. Together we own Bon Ami, which is of course French for good friend, and I had a lot of those at the races. I can't remember signing so many autographs or having as many photographs taken by fans and well-wishers. Just before the Cup, in an interview with Leslie Graham, I said that the Ayr Gold Cup was

Tommy Doherty's So Careful with jockey Nicky Carlisle and JB

my favourite race, and I would love to win it again, although it wouldn't be the end of the world if we didn't, as my lifelong ambition had already been fulfilled. Having been there, done that and got the T-shirt, one shouldn't be too greedy. I can retire a man satisfied. Bon Ami ran a great race to finish ninth, only beaten three and a half lengths.

Nowadays, racing's supremo, Peter Savill, has us working on the Sabbath. Although I had to forgo my roast beef and Yorkshire pudding to go to Newcastle, I did not see the Sunday-racing lover there on 19 September. In fact, I haven't seen him at race meetings on any of the holy days. He says we need Sunday racing but he certainly isn't speaking on my behalf, and I certainly don't think he is acting in the best interests of the majority of racing's workforce.

At Gosforth Park, very little atmosphere was generated by the small crowd. Mind you, the day was not planned very well, as Newcastle United, with their great army of supporters, were playing at home against Sheffield Wednesday. The only time there was any excitement at the races was when Newcastle scored, prompting loud cheers. As the

Magpies won 8–0, this was quite often. Alan Shearer scored five of the goals, making a dry rub for the Owls. It reminded me of the England versus Germany game three years ago, when it was shown live on the big screen at Kempton and Chester, where I was. When Shearer scored the goal, the crowd cheered so loudly that the horses were spooked. At Kempton a jockey was unseated before a race.

On our way home, Paul Bradley and I called at Newcastle General, to see how jump jockey Scott Taylor was getting on. Scott had a very nasty fall in a novice chase at Perth on 20 August. He received serious head injuries and was taken to Ninewell Hospital, Dundee in a coma. To make it easier for his family and friends to visit, Scott was later transferred to Newcastle General, where he had no shortage of visitors. The day Paul and I popped in, he already had a number of jump jockeys in, on their way to and from Kelso races. Ex-jockeys John Leach and Phil Tuck were arriving just as we were leaving. There are lots of regular race meetings around that part of the country and many people pass on their way to the Scottish courses, so Scott can be sure of having a lot of company.

The following Monday, at 7.58 a.m., I caught the rattler to London for my second meeting in my capacity as trustee of the Injured Jockeys Fund at 42 Portman Square, where I was made TPR for Scott Taylor, having already acquired Ray Peacock. I can assure all the generous people who support the Injured Jockeys Fund that their money is spent very wisely. Every case is forwarded by sensible almoners, and the trustees have regular meetings to decide on what, where and to whom the money goes. In case of emergencies, the almoners get on to the case and action starts immediately. Although I have not been in my new role very long, I am enjoying the experience.

17

What a Day That Was!

The Irish Fairyhouse Yearling Sales were on 21 and 22 September. Alan went with his mother (to hold his hand, as it were). I stayed at home and held the fort. When Jo rang later on in the day, I said, 'Right, mate, what have you bought?'

'Two cups of coffee and a bacon butty!' came the reply.

I bet those Irish vendors and auctioneers were chuffed to bits with my two big spenders. Tomorrow the pair have another day on the loose, so we shall see how they fare then.

During the second day of the sales, as Sam and I are on our way to Leicester races, The Bride rings me to tell me that she and Alan have got off the brakes and given nine thousand Irish punts for a filly by Goldmark. They have also seen a nice colt by Mind Games (Dennis), which looks just like him.

'If you like the horse, buy him,' I said. 'And let's hope that he's as good as his dad.'

While I was at Chester, Jo rang again. They didn't buy the Dennis lookalike, or anything else for that matter, and were making their way home. I just wish I could trust her like that with the clothes shops. Had it been a clothes sale, no doubt she would have bought half a dozen new outfits.

Our two-year-old, Glenrock, ran well in the nursery with top weight of nine stone seven pounds, finishing third, beaten four lengths by Myttons Again, giving him thirty pounds. The winner was trained by Alan Bailey and ridden by our apprentice, Iona Wands. Jokingly, Alan said to me that it's been so long since any of his horses had won, he expected a stewards' enquiry as to why he'd trained a winner. Immediately after the fourth race, Bobby McAlpine, the course chairman, presented me with a magnum of champagne as a farewell gift. I asked Bobby for glasses, to

JB filling up the glasses at Chester

share the bottle with the punters round the winner's enclosure. Bobby did a bit of spiel about yours truly on the mike and passed it on to me to say a few words. I was about to say we have had a lot of fun at Chester where there is always a great buzz, when some punter shouted, 'Sing us "The Jolly Farmer", Jack.' Although I am game for most things, I cocked a deaf 'un there.

I was asked to do another interview on the Racing Channel. The punters sitting on their armchairs at home must be sick of the sight of me. When our other runner, Palacegate Touch, alias Archie, was walking round the paddock, I was just about to give the lad a mild roasting for not plaiting his mane when Raymond Corbett, the race sponsor, came up to the lad with an envelope and said, 'Congratulations, young man. You have just won fifty pounds for the best turned-out horse.' You just can't get it right!

The very next day the armchair punters must have nearly had a wobbler, seeing me on their screens yet again. This time at Pontefract, talking to Alex Hammond, just before our only runner, Bolshaya, finished second, beaten half a length. Jo had been chatting to Les Eyre, the Hambleton trainer, who said, 'Have you found anywhere to retire to yet?' We are not desperate, but we do want a place with a few acres, so that we are not in Alan's hair forever. Les then told Jo about a property at Sutton Bank, with about nine acres, and kindly said that we could use his gallops for our jumpers.

After the racing, Jo and I went to see the place, but it wasn't our scene. We made our way to Les's yard, the very place where Julie Cecil was born, and Les gave us a tour of his gallops. We all ended up in Les's local, the Hambleton Inn, which belongs to Captain Harry Barlow, the proud owner of Swan At Whalley, which we trained. We had just ordered our meal when Kevin Ryan, who used to be our second head-man and is now a successful trainer at Hambleton, came in. Over a couple of jars we had a great night. We had to decline Kevin's offer of a bed as tomorrow we have runners at Haydock, Redcar and Lingfield, not to mention six horses going to Doncaster's horses-in-training sale, to make room for some yearlings.

At our local meeting on Saturday, 23 September at Haydock, our two-year-old Kanaka Creek ran second, beaten just half a length in the heavy ground into a position we have filled too many times of late. John Carroll did say he should have won, as he went well clear a furlong out, but his arse was alight and he couldn't wait, which meant he got collared close to home. At the time of writing, we have trained eighty-seven seconds against sixty-six winners. A few years ago we were having a run of seconds. In the tea bar, before racing at Doncaster, I was chatting to Graham Lyle, the Leeds bookie, a smashing man I have known for years. 'You're having a good season, Jack. You look nailed on for a hundred winners,' he said.

'I don't know about that, mate. We look nailed on for a hundred seconds.'

'You can have 33–1 against that happening,' he said.

I think he was trying to brighten me up.

'For a fun bet, let me have a ton on at fifties,' I said.

'Go on then,' said Graham.

On the last York meeting that year, Graham presented me with a cheque for five thousand pounds, in the second's enclosure. For sure, I wasn't complaining about having seconds that day.

JB being presented with a cheque at York

I listened to Kanaka's Creek's race on my mobile, on the way to Scotland where Jo and I were attending a dinner in my honour, hosted by Musselburgh racecourse. We booked into the Robbie Burns Hotel in Joppa, where we changed into our evening gear, as it was a black-tie do.

All the proceeds from the auction, sports quiz and singalong were going to the Injured Jockeys Holiday Fund. Fran Marshall and Bill Tarnworth worked so hard to put the show on and it was brilliant. Henry Beeby was master of ceremonies and auctioneer and embarrassed me no end with his over-the-top flattering speech.

Lucinda Russell, Jim Goldie, Hazel Dudgeon, John Budden, Mark Kershaw and John Berry were the panel for the racing quiz. The first question was, 'What was the name of Jack Berry's first winner, and what was the racecourse?' John Budden was spot-on with Camasco at Kelso. The auction had some excellent lots on offer and raised £3,140. I am sure that if Ron Huggins, Trigger's owner, had seen the beautiful painting of Double Trigger by Jenny Lupton, he would have made a serious bid. The dinner, in traditional Yorkshire style, was roast beef and Yorkshire pudding. Peter Collins, the Scottish bookie, took bets on the

151

Peter Collins and JB – the punter's pal

quiz. He brought his board, on which he had painted 'Jack Berry – the Punters' Pal', to price up the event.

We had a great night, and to finish off, I led everyone in a singsong. We all sang 'The Grand Old Duke of York', which was a lot of fun. In the second verse, we missed out the ups, and all the people who said up had to pay a five-pound forfeit. Then we missed out all the downs, then the ups and the downs. Auctioneer Mouse White couldn't get it right and had to cough up the limit, ten pounds. It's incredible how people rally round for good causes. In all, the venture made over six thousand pounds and we had a great night. Jo and I got back to our hotel at around 2.00 a.m.

Frances and Jimmy Jack, our Scottish friends of many years, came to the Robbie Burns Hotel on Sunday morning to have breakfast with us as they were over from America on holiday, having emigrated there in 1984.

Jimmy was good pals with another of our owners, Albert Waring, who played rugby for Wigan and England in the sixties. One day, Jimmy was confiding in Albert that he thought I was hyperactive, saying, 'Do you know, the other day Jack fed the horses first thing, mucked out the front yard and rode out before the other lads had even started work?' The pair of prats, unknown to me, made an apppointment with a shrink, whom Albert knew well. They conned me into going by telling me this Dr Shuni, who lived near Southport, wanted to buy a horse. When I went to his house, Dr Shuni showed me into a room. He asked me about my riding days and how long I had been training. We then went into another room and he said, 'Sit down there, Jack, there's something I want you to listen to,' then buggered off. At first there was a noise like waves swishing about, then faint soothing music. A man's soft voice whispered, 'R–E–L–A–X, R–E–L–A–X. Your whole body is getting lighter and lighter.' I was looking round for the controls to switch the crap off, but couldn't, as it was coming through the speakers, high on the walls. The voice said, 'You are now fully relaxed. You feel drowsy.' (No, I'm not, I thought, and I can't see this nut buying a horse, either.) Sometime later the silly beggar came back into the room. He said nothing about buying a yearling but handed me a tape and told me, 'After lunch each day I want you to lie on your bed and play this cassette.' When I got back to the car, Jo and Jimmy were waiting for me. I played hell with Jimmy: 'Don't you think I have better things to bloody do?' After a while I started to come round, and said, 'I'm glad he hadn't locked the door, at least he let me out.' Mischievously, Jimmy said, 'Put the tape on, Jack. Let's hear it.' It soon had us in stitches – and within a few minutes, Jo was fast asleep. It became a standing joke in the yard. When I wasn't about, the lads would say, 'Is the boss lying in bed listening to his tape?'

We were laughing so much reminiscing about the old times in the breakfast room, that I bet the staff were glad when I 'weighed-in' with the bill and they saw the back of us.

At Musselburgh, all the races had names relating to the Injured Jockeys Holiday Fund: the Jack Berry Injured Jockeys Holiday Fund Maiden, the One Hundred Grand Target Nursery Stakes, the Bid For The Red Shirt Stakes, the Jolly Farmer Handicap, the Thank You Fran Stakes and lastly the Fund-Raising Maestro Handicap Stakes. As we had plenty of time before before the races, we went to Leith Docks to the

Jimmy Jack and JB on the Royal Yacht Brittania

Britannia Centre to have a guided tour of the Royal Yacht *Britannia*, which was fabulous. It's amazing to think that the yacht has sailed one million miles in its forty-three years of service, carrying members of our royal family and countless notable men and women all over the world. I felt honoured to be aboard.

Sadly we didn't have enough time to take it all in as we had to get back to Musselburgh where we had two runners in the first race. They finished third and fourth behind Jaybirds. I presented the winning connections with a trophy. After the third race, one of my red shirts was auctioned by John Budden. The bidding went to a hundred and eighty pounds when the punters started to ask for the shirt on my back, rather than the ringer. I changed shirts and John continued the bidding, which ended up at three hundred pounds. After the Jolly Farmer Handicap, I gave the large crowd a rendition of the song.

Fittingly, our mare Best of All, owned by Robert Aird and ridden by Gary Carter, won the Thank You Fran race, as Fran had worked tirelessly setting the day up. I signed dozens of autographs, had lots of photos taken with punters, did an interview with BBC Radio Scotland and yes, yet another slot on the Racing Channel with Gordon Brown. What a fun Sunday we all had in brilliant sunshine. Peter Savill doesn't know what he missed!

As it was Hamilton the next day, it didn't make sense to travel home only to return to Scotland a few hours later. Jo and I went with trainer Linda Perratt and her parents, Helen and George, to Jasmine One, a Chinese restaurant at Giffnock, owned by Peter Tsim whose Sha-Tin Venture is trained by Linda. We had a great banquet and stayed over at the Perratts.

To kill a bit of time before the races, Jo and I went into the town's pet shop and bought a few things for my dogs. Seeing the small animals there reminded me of a time when Alan and Sam were kids. I had bought them a hamster and the whole family set off for the pet shop in Doncaster to buy a cage. Jo waited in the car with the excited youngsters while I went into the shop, where I was told that I would find the cages upstairs. There sitting at a table was a women sorting mice into perspex trays. Seated on the table to her left was a very small, innocent-looking monkey. I told the woman that I wanted a hamster cage with a wheel and she went into another room. Being friendly to the monkey, I said, 'Hello, mate. Aren't you a little cracker! What's your name?' The monkey stood up and took the cardboard lid off one of the perspex trays; then, looking at me as if butter would not melt in its mouth, it started flicking the mice out of the tray. 'No, no, don't do that, little fellow,' I said, but it took no notice. 'Don't do that! Stop it!' I pleaded. 'Stop it, you little prat.' As I walked towards it, the darned thing ran round the table tipping the trays up. I began straightening the trays and trying to put the mice back, getting them all mixed up in the process. Then the monkey started to throw a tantrum, making all sorts of shrieking noises. By now there were effing mice all over the place. The woman came back after few minutes with the cage in her hand and saw the pandemonium.

'What on earth are you doing,' she yelled at me.

'Me doing – it's that bloody monkey,' I tried to tell her, feeling sure that someone was going to stick a mike in my face at any moment and say, 'You are on *Candid Camera*.'

'Get out! Get out!' the woman screamed behind me as I flew down the stairs and out through the shop. People must have thought I was a robber or a rapist as I dived into my car and sped off with the woman still shrieking after me. Jo and the kids were demanding to know where the cage was, but for some time I was laughing too much to be able to explain.

In those days, I did all the driving. Until we started training in the rented yard at Arksey, Jo did not even attempt to pass her test. You could hardly say she was a natural as she did not pass until her fourth attempt. On her first go she failed for not taking enough care at road junctions. The second time, she hit a car on a roundabout and the examiner was so anxious to get out of the car that he forgot to fill in the form giving the reasons for the failure. On my mate's third try she failed for not looking in her rear mirror enough and not paying sufficient attention at junctions. After her fourth and this time success-ful attempt she rang up her mother, who was staying with us at the time, to tell her the good news. When we came back into the yard from riding out, waving about on the clothes line was a towel with the words 'Congratulations! Jo has passed her test!' emblazoned across it, pro-claiming her triumph.

On my return from Hamilton's last race meeting of the season, my car boot was laden with four bottles of spirits, two presents and five cards which racegoers had given me for my retirement. It's all very touching and I do appreciate it.

On Tuesday, 28 September, at Sedgefield, we ran one of our rare jumpers, ridden by A. P. McCoy. As I put the tack on Amlwch, the Racing Channel scout was hovering around waiting for me.

'Don't say you want me on the box again?'

'Yes, please. Alex Hammond said would you come on as it isn't often we get you with a runner at a jump meeting.'

I said, 'Tell Alex that I am definitely not going on. Folk will be sick of the sight of me.'

Owned and bred by one of our long-standing patrons, Lord Mostyn, a dream to train for, who in years gone by used to train himself, Amlwch, the 4–7 favourite, duly won the novice hurdle.

'Surely you will come on now,' said the scout. Needless to say, I gave in, knowing that it is always fun being on with the bubbly Mrs H, who knows how to make an interview lively and interesting.

Bob Bowden, the course chairman, invited Jo and me to his box for a drink. After racing we drove on to Newcastle General to visit Scott Taylor, who I thought looked a better colour than when I last saw him. He also apeared to have a little feeling in his right hand, which he didn't have before. Scott is far from well, but any sign of improvement at this stage is welcome. Cyril Greenland, the Northern declarations clerk, along with starter's assistant and ex-jockey Mac Turner, started a fund for Scott last week at the races and they have already received over three thousand pounds. Scott will be taken good care of by the Injured Jockeys Fund if he lives until he is a hundred, whatever his needs. People may not realise that there is no limit to the help the IJF give. In fact around six thousand pounds per week is distributed in benefits.

On Wednesday, 29 September, I had a phonecall from the Racing Channel inviting me to be their guest for the day on the 13 October at Haydock Park, which would have been a nice little earner. Unfortunately, I couldn't accept as the Newmarket yearling sales are on and there is a filly by Pivotal related to our Bolshoi that I would nearly kill for.

Neville, our feed man, and I paid a visit to Old Trafford where Manchester United defeated Olympic de Marseille 2–1. United were down at half-time, but they fought back like tigers to get the result. After the game, in the VIP lounge, Alex, as you can imagine, was in great form. Someone told a great story about Jack Charlton. He was reputed to be tight and would often cash cheques for very small amounts, knowing that a lot of people would be more likely to frame a cheque signed by a footballing legend than bank it!

You could say that I have done a few different jobs in racing in my time, but the first day of October took a bit of beating. I was asked to auction, in between races at Hexham, some beautifully framed land-scapes by Derek Taylor. Mr Taylor is a big fan of the Injured Jockeys Fund and wanted its chairman, Lord Oaksey, to do the business. Unfortunately the good lord had other commitments and I was asked to act as super-sub. In his letter asking me to do the job, Charles Endersby, the Clerk of the Course, had written, 'It should be a very enjoyable day,' but it had rained all night and was still peeing down when I got to the track. The bookies started to leave after the second race. After the fourth race, a selling hurdle, the winner's enclosure was deserted and there was no bid for the winner. Charles Endersby rather sheepishly asked me if we should postpone the auction of the paintings, as there was nobody there. I could have hugged him. Had punters been watching from the stand they probably would have thought it was Gene Kelly making a comeback. My two-hundred-and-nineteen-mile round trip was a waste of time, though I am sure that Scott Taylor and many others would love to have been in my position and able to do it.

On the way home it was still raining heavily when I stopped at the Little Chef car park about six miles from Hexham to listen on my yuppee phone to our Red Typhoon win another claimer at Lingfield.

Nearer home I heard on the radio that the soft French have not passed our beef as fit to eat. Later, as Jo was away, I grilled myself a thick juicy English rib-eye steak that must have weighed a pound, and served it along with some onions, oven-ready chips and sugar-snap peas. I opened a bottle of 1996 Californian Cabernet Sauvignon and, with all my dogs sitting around, I poured my first glass. Great, I'm thinking. Balls to the French!

Halfway through my steak the phone rang. It was The Captain, John Brown, speaking very quietly.

'Are you all right, mate?' I asked, knowing full well that his missus, Vera, had been very poorly for months, and dreading the worst.

'Vera has passed away. I was with her when she went. I don't know when it will be, but will you and Jo come to the funeral? She loved you and Jo, you know that.' Poor old John couldn't manage to get any more out and put the phone down.

This summer, since Angie Baby got claimed at Bath, we haven't seen much of our Sam, as he's been stopping quite a lot with Carole Phillips in Oxfordshire. Carole cooks for Henry Candy's lads. She and Sam get on ever so well together. I wish something constructive would come out of it as they are good for each other. She takes Sam all over the place. Tonight she rang me to tell me that tomorrow they are going

My birthday bash at the Cottage Restaurant

to Devon for the weekend. Sam comes home to Cockerham on Monday, then on Wednesday he flies back to his apartment in Tenerife for the winter.

On Thursday, 7 October, I was sixty-two years old. Even at this age, birthdays give me quite a buzz. No less than twenty-four people sent cards and faxes, plus I got a few phonecalls from people who had read it in the *Racing Post*. In the evening, my old lady took me out to the Cottage Restaurant, in Goosnargh, near Preston. It's a small family-run place with no licence to sell wine or spirits, so we take our own. Bede and Agnes Rogerson, the proprietors, are friendly with us. We had arranged to meet Ruth and John Barrett and Anne Hartley at the restaurant and together we enjoyed lobster thermidor followed by venison with our red wine. Bede brought in a lovely home-made birthday cake with *Happy Birthday* written in icing and just one candle. Every time I blew it out, it relit, which made us all fall about laughing. We had a super night but I will remember when its Jo's birthday to keep off the pop and drive the car like she did.

The next day, although we didn't have any runners, I went to Carlisle for a day's jumping and to do an interview with Peter Scudamore for the *Daily Mail*. In Saturday's *Sun* there was a two-page write-up by Claude Duval, racing journalist of the year, which said that racing's most famous colours were not Godolphin's, Sheikh Mohammed's or Fahd Salman's, but my selection of bright red shirts. Claude went on to say that I had been to Windsor Castle, patted the corgis and taken part in the Royal Ascot procession. All true – and what a day that was, I can tell you!

It all started when Lieutenant Colonel Sir Guy Acland, the Queen's Deputy Master of the Household, sent an invitation to Jo and me to lunch with the Queen and Prince Philip at Windsor Castle on the Friday of Royal Ascot in 1996. To get the timing right we did a trial run to Windsor Castle in the car before racing started as the last thing we wanted was to be late. On the other hand, we did not want to be too early, either. On the day, we hadn't bargained with the police closing the roads that led from Ascot to the Castle and making it a one-way system. We had to follow the detour and drive farther and a bit faster than we had originally intended, reaching the palace right on cue with not a minute to spare.

The Queen, the Queen Mum, the Duchess of Kent and the Duke of Edinburgh were wonderful. There were about eighteen people in all for lunch and the royals chatted to all of us. After lunch, we were led down a long corridor, with beautiful paintings on either side. The corgis belonging to the Queen and the Queen Mother were jogging along beside us, which created a homely atmosphere. It was so amusing when the Queen Mum went left, her corgis broke away from the pack and followed her, while the others carried on with the Queen.

We were driven from Windsor Castle in the royal cars to meet the horse-drawn carriages. In our carriage was the Honourable Caroline Nevile (Lady Derby to be) and the Honourable Mrs Marten, along with French racing supremo, M. Louis Romanet. As we drove along the roads, people were waving. When we went through the golden gates and up the centre of Ascot's straight mile, what a buzz that was! The stalls team were waiting for the coach with me in it and as we approached the five-furlong start, they let out a spirited cheer – 'Good

PHOTOGRAPH: BERNARD PARKIN

JB in the royal carriage with the Honourable Caroline Nevile, the
Honourable Mrs Marten and M. Louis Romanet

old Jack!' As if that wasn't embarrassing enough, as our carriage went through the iron gates to enter the paddock enclosure, there were more cheers. Mrs Marten said, 'Now I know how it must feel to be with a pop star.'

It would have been nice to have a winner on that momentous day, but it wasn't to be. Dennis was odds-on favourite for the King's Stand Stakes but could only finish third to Mick Channon's Piccolo. For all that, it was a great day, one which Jo and I will never forget.

Claude Duval went a bit OTT when he quoted me as saying, 'I used to marvel at trainers going on winter holidays to Barbados while I was at home getting my two-year-olds revved up for Doncaster. Now I go there myself for three months.' In your dreams, Claude! But he was accurate in saying that I reinforced my royal connections by receiving an MBE from the Queen. That was a moment to cherish. One night, I received a phonecall asking me if I was offered an award would I accept it, as my

JB with the Queen

name had been put forward. I was not too sure if it was a wind-up, but the voice sounded genuine. 'Certainly – in fact, I would be delighted,' I said. I was told that I would get a letter and then have to ring to confirm that the letter was in my possession. I was sworn to secrecy until the honour was announced in the press.

On the eve of the investiture, Jo and I stayed at Durrants Hotel in London. In the evening we went to the theatre with the Deuters, who were living in London at that time, to see the Lloyd Webber musical *By Jeeves* – only I didn't see too much of it, as the woman in front of me sported a beehive hairstyle which looked like a guardsman's busby. Had she been a horse she would have been a prime candidate for a worming, as she couldn't keep still for two minutes!

Next morning, a chauffeur-driven limo floated the four of us off to Buckingham Palace where the ceremony look place in absolute splendour, with an orchestra playing beautiful music throughout the whole ceremony. The feeling was one of being in a dreamworld. When I approached the Queen for my award, she remarked favourably on my

PHOTOGRAPH: JOHN STILLWELL, PA NEWS

JB and Jo outside Buckingham Palace

red shirt. She asked how the season was going and said that she was delighted to be giving me the medal. Jo and I posed for the traditional photos outside the palace.

To give the finishing touch to the most perfect day, Jo, Chris, Antonia and I went to the Ritz to celebrate with a champagne lunch fit for a king, kindly arranged by the Deuters.

On Saturday, 9 October we had another fabulous day. A few weeks beforehand, John Smith, York's Clerk of the Course, asked me to send him a list of about thirty friends I would like to invite to a party in honour of my retirement. The invitations were sent out by York's chairman, Lord Halifax.

Chairman's Lunch
Saturday 9 October 1999
To mark the retirement of Mr Jack Berry MBE

Clantime

Earl of Halifax
Mrs J. Berry
Mr P. Farrell
Mrs P. Farrell
Mr C. Deuters
Mrs R. E. Howard-Vyse
Mr J. N. Gundill
Mrs G. Blum
Mr W. Wharton

So Careful

Countess of Halifax
Mr J. Berry
Mrs J. N. Gundill
Mrs T. Bibby
Mr G. Blum
Miss G. Campion
Mr J. Heler
Mrs W. Wharton
Lord Oaksey

Mind Games

Mr S. E. Scrope
Lady Oaksey
Mr A. Berry
Mrs N. H. T. Wrigley
Mr C. Nutter
Mrs C. Deuters
Mr T. Bibby
Miss L. Blum
Mrs J. Forsyth

Paris House

Mr R. E. Howard-Vyse
Mrs J. Heler
Mr T. Holdcroft
Mrs C. Nutter
Miss S. Townley
Mr T. McWilliams
Mrs T. McWilliams
Mr J. Forsyth
Mrs T. Holdcroft

Lord Halifax presents JB with the solid-silver salver

It was very good of York, who looked after us so well all day. We had a champagne reception and, as you can see from the seating plan, the tables were named after four of our best horses. The weather kept fine, it was good racing and we had a brilliant time. After the Rockingham Stakes, Lord Halifax presented Jo and me with a very nice solid-silver salver. Lilo Blum travelled all the way from Spain to attend. Mary Farrell complimented me on my two-day-old haircut. Although her hubby Paddy wasn't very well, he wouldn't let me get the doctor to him, saying he would see his own doctor when he returned home. I rang him at about 9.00 p.m. to see how he was. Geraldine, his daughter, told me her dad was fine but they had just received some bad news. Paddy's sister Kitty had had a heart attack at a football match in Ireland and died in the ambulance on the way to hospital.

18

Talk About People Being Generous . . .

On Monday, 11 October, the black tie came out again as Jo and I went to Vera Brown's funeral in Worsley, near Manchester. A lot of people came, as Vera was very well liked. Afterwards there was food and drink at Worsley's Old Hall, which is said to date from the Conquest.

The following day The Bride and I were guests of Ayr racecourse chairman, Donald MacQuaker. The racecourse had named races after those two old sweats, Peter Calver, who is also retiring from training at the end of the season, and yours truly. My race, the Jack Berry Retirement Stakes, was over a mile and five furlongs. No end of people said to me, 'Fancy having a race named after you and it not being a sprint!' Even Richard Pridham, Clerk of the Course, apologised for the race not being a dash, so the punters must have been getting at him too. But it is nice to have a race of any sort named after you, and Peter and I both appreciated it.

As soon as the weighed-in signal had sounded after my race, John Budden gave a speech about my career, after which Donald MacQuaker presented me with a very nice silver dish. It would have been great to have won the race with Garnock Valley, our last runner on the course I love, but the old boy had to settle for the runner-up spot. And yes, Gordon Brown had me say a few words on the box.

Willie Morgan rang me on my yuppie on my way back to Newmarket on Thursday to invite me to lunch in his box at Haydock Park. I told Willie that I wished I could but I was on my way to Newmarket in horrendous traffic. The two-hundred-and-thirty-mile journey took just under five hours. At the sales, trade was vibrant. Any sharp, precocious yearlings were making far more than they were worth. Gerry Blum's sister Lilo was champing at the bit for a racey type around the eight- to twelve-thousand-guinea bracket, but we kept on getting blown away. I had set my heart on Lot 450, a filly from David and Trish Brown's Furnace Mill Stud, which had taken my eye when I visited the stud before the sales. She was a very sharp-looking filly by Pivotal, the horse that beat our Mind Games in the 1996 King's Stand Stakes. Her second dam, Mainly Dry, bred Bolshoi, last year's King's Stand winner, as well as Tod, the only horse to beat champion sprinter Dayjur as a three-year-old, and Brocklesby winner Great Chaddington, all of whom had been trained at Cockerham. Facing fierce opposition from Julie Camacho, we had the final nod at forty-five thousand guineas. Right away, Lilo wanted to take a quarter share in the filly. If Lilo was married to Sheikh Mohammed, he would have twice as many horses in training! Let's hope the filly makes it to the Queen Mary, as I have a real gut-feeling for this one.

On Friday Jo and I again met dreadful traffic on our way down to Newmarket, getting there just five minutes before the first yearling, Lot 303, was due to be sold. This was the main yearling for me in the day's sale, a filly by Mujadil, a half-sister to For Old Times' Sake, a horse we trained for Gerry Blum to win six races. As I was looking at the filly in the inspection pen, agent David Redfern said to me: 'I am going to buy her for one of your owners!'

'Are you sure,' I said, 'because I have got an owner interested and there is no point in making her expensive one for the other.' David told me Chris and Antonia Deuters had commissioned him to buy a nice sharp filly and he had chosen her. Sure enough, David secured her for twenty-seven thousand guineas.

Gerry and Bridget Blum, Ken Ivory, Valerie Hubbard, Jo and I all went to the White Heart in Tuddenham for a splendid meal. There we met up with Ivor Markham, a fellow rider of mine in the past but now a race-reader and reporter. After the meal I asked mine host for a doggy bag for the left-over bones as a treat for my dog Bandit. I suggested that we all put a fiver in the kitty and guess the weight of the bones, the winner splitting forty pounds with the Injured Jockeys Fund. Estimates covered a wide range but Ivor got it spot on with one pound ten ounces.

Sportingly, he gave me the twenty pounds back, so the fund benefited by forty pounds and we all had a lot of fun.

On my return from Newmarket there was a nice fax from the Injured Jockeys Fund chief executive, Jeremy Richardson, sent on behalf of Lord Oaksey, confirming arrangements for us to have lunch with the Queen Mum at the Goring Hotel on 2 December, a pleasure we had the honour of three years ago at the same venue, not long after she had had an operation to remove a fishbone from her throat. The first course turned out to be fish, and as I had the privilege of sitting next to the gracious lady, I could not help wondering what I would do if she swallowed another fishbone. What a wonderful and knowledgeable person she is. We all had a great day with her and I am looking forward to my next lunch in her company.

Talk about people being generous! Neil Midgley the football referee and I auctioned some forty items people had kindly donated in aid of the Scott Taylor Appeal Fund. Arrangements had been made by Kevin Ryan and Les Eyre at the Whitestonecliff, a pub near Sutton Bank. The evening raised over ten thousand pounds. Tony Fawcett, better known for being the proud owner of Benzoe, was particularly generous, buying several lots.

On Monday at Pontefract our only runner was balloted out. Jo and I went along anyhow, as lunch guests of race sponsor, Jack Clayton.

I was telling Jackie O'Neill about an electronic system I had heard about which, by use of a special collar, prevented dogs straying off the premises.

'I wonder if that would work to keep our bull mastiff in a pen now that the baby can crawl. I just don't trust him,' Jackie said.

'You're joking,' I said, but I could see that she was worried. The dog was about six years old and had therefore been in the yard before the nipper was born and so was bound to be a bit jealous. 'Give me your vet's phone number,' I said, which she did. Then I turned to Jonjo, Jackie's other half, and told him, 'I'm getting your dog put down, if that's all right!'

'Go ahead,' he replied. 'Jackie worries in case the dog bites the young fellow, and, to be honest, we have been thinking about it.'

A Scott Taylor Appeal Fund evening

So I did. There and then, on my mobile. As I was leaving, one of the other guests said to me: 'I know where to go now when someone wants to get rid of a dog!'

On Wednesday, 20 October, Charlie Lambert of BBC Northwest came along with a cameraman at 8.00 a.m. to film a day in my life, to be shown on television on 4 November. First of all we worked the horses and filmed the runners being loaded into the horsebox *en route* to Newcastle. Then Charlie came with me in the car to the races. Kieren Fallon, who needed just one winner to make his double century for the season, rode our Bolshaya, the 5–1 favourite. It would have been great to help Kieren reach that milestone but unfortunately the filly finished in the middle.

Alan and I attended the Doncaster October Yearling Sale, where the young lad bought a couple of sharp sorts by King's Signet and Presidium, for six thousand and three thousand five hundred guineas respectively. There was a time when we would have bought a dozen or more of these types, but in those days there would have been a lot more races for them to run in. Alongside Alan at the sales were a number of other young

Alan and JB at Doncaster Races

hopefuls, including Jamie Osborne, John Weymes, Tim Fitzgerald and Sylvester Kirk. They were all looking for bargains and clients to buy for. They need instant success to get going and that means two-year-olds.

To be honest, I don't think there has ever been a harder time to start up training as now. Having said that, it's never been easy. Years ago, I remember discussing the subject with an old Yorkshireman, when I was first thinking of training. He said: 'Tha needs luck, and lots of it, to make a go of training hosses. Ah would buy 'em, ah would sell 'em, ah would back 'em, ah would lay 'em, ah would ride 'em, ah would even eat the buggers, but nay to 'ell, ah wouldn't train 'em.'

On Friday morning Alan and I bought two more yearlings before going over the road to the races.

The Red-Shirt Brigade manager, Peter Murphy, had hired a box for the day and around thirty members attended. Red Typhoon, the club's filly, ran in the Doncaster October Yearling Sale's Race without troubling the judge. In fact she only beat four of the eighteen runners. Don Buckley, a

Red-Shirt member, said to me, 'How did the handicapper justify putting her up fourteen pounds for winning that claimer at Haydock?'

'Mr Tester is here today,' I said, 'go and ask him.' Which he did. When Don saw me later, he said, 'What's Mr Tester's initial? D?' Don said that he had owned horses for sixteen years and it was a waste of time talking to him as he got no joy at all from the conversation.

In the afternoon, Jo and I went to the Doncaster Sale's box for a bite to eat and a drink. We watched our Garnock Valley win the sprint at Newbury on their TV, and I can assure you that we were not the only ones shouting Garnock home. At the sale's evening session, we Berrys bought six yearlings between us. Afterwards, Jo and I were dinner guests of the sale's boss, Harry Beeby. I was drawn between Linda Perratt and Liz Beeby, which was great fun.

The following Tuesday, on the way back from Bath races, where our sole runner was unplaced, Jo and I called in to see Ray Peacock. In April, Ray had a terrible fall exercising a horse on the gallops and received horrendous paralysing injuries, fracturing his neck, some vertebrae and ribs. His neck was broken so badly that it had to be stabilised with some bone from his thigh. He must have wondered if he would ever walk again. After months of hospital treatment, Ray is now at home again, but still goes to hospital four times a week for physiotherapy. Thank goodness, through sheer guts, determination and family support, Ray is well on the mend.

On Thursday, 28 October, on my way to Sedgefield races to see Amlwch run, Jo gave me quite a shock. She told me that she and Liz Cameron are only coming to London with our party for the stable lads boxing! It wouldn't be so bad if they actually came to watch the stable lads getting rid of a bit of aggression, but they are going shopping.

Barrie Hunter, an equestrian sales rep, called in to see if he could sell me any of his wares. One of his lines was some black-leather head-collars. In conversation, he was telling me that he had been to Harvey and Sue Smith's, where Barrie had shown them to Sue.

Harvey, a true down-to-earth Yorkshireman, who wouldn't spend a penny if half a one would do, saw the head-collars and said: 'I can get them a lot cheaper than that.'

'How do you know, I haven't told you the price yet,' said Barrie.

'Tha won't match my price. Four for a pound I can get 'em for, with a rope on.'

'Wherever from,' said Barrie.

'The local knacker man,' Harvey replied. 'All the horses go there with a head-collar and he has ner use fer 'em.'

Sue said, 'Take no notice of the silly beggar,' and bought some.

Three weeks ago, Bill Robinson, proprietor of the Talbot at Bishopton, near Sedgefield, rang me to see if I would accept from him a full set of Martell Grand National water jugs from 1989–99, in mint condition, and auction them at any function I saw fit, with the proceeds to go to the Injured Jockeys Fund. Bill is a loyal supporter of the fund and friendly with jump jockey Andrew Thornton, who is a native of Bishopton. Bill told me that his wife was ill, and after twenty-six years in the pub, he was calling it a day. After racing at Sedgefield, Jo and I went to the Talbot, where Bill had arranged for us to have a very nice meal with a few of his friends and to pick up the beautiful collector's pieces. Unfortunately, since our first conversation, Bill's wife, Elaine, had died, so it was nice for him to have his pals around for support.

Talk about the way to grow mushrooms is to keep them in the dark and feed them plenty of muck! Until this Saturday, two days before the entries close for Doncaster's last Flat meeting of the season, I didn't know that our owners had sponsored a race and named it The Big Thank You To Jack And Jo Lady Riders' Champion Stakes. It's great how staff can keep quiet about some things. Had it been a horse burning up the gallops, everyone would have known!

It's amazing how one has to drag information out of staff at times, and the subtle way they let you have the news. A few years ago, coming back after several hours off the premises, I asked the secretary who worked for us at that time if there had been anything exciting that day.

'No, not really,' she replied.

'Anyone rung, anyone been, anything happened, any problems?' I asked.

The lady in question, all in one breath, said something like this: 'The vet came and cut two horses. John Brown rang, wanting to know if you

JB and friends at the pub with the Martell water jugs

intend to run Mammas Too at Newbury. Willie Lefebre rang to ask if you are fixed up with a jockey for Gorinsky at Ayr. Mark Tompkins rang to say that you had left your coat at his house when you were there last week. Your dad died. Ian the accountant wants you to give him a ring. Terry Holdcroft called in to see his horses, as he was passing. As you will see on the car park, a load of woodchip came for the gallop. A dog bit the postman. That's all – oh, and I will be in a bit late tomorrow as I am going to the dentist.'

Now in its thirty-fourth year, the stable lads' boxing night was held at the London Hilton on 1 November, with Martin Pipe as the guest of honour. As usual, the boxing was good, though there are not nearly as many lads who want to box nowadays, probably on account of the lack of training facilities. I know the club our lads used to train at in Lancaster has closed, which means they would have to go now to Preston, which is miles away. Hence we had no runners. In 1992, three of our boxers got through to the finals. Paul Fessey beat Jason

Alan Daly v. Carl Lowther – stable lads' boxing night 1992

Wilkinson, from Lord Huntington's yard, and Alan Daly beat our other apprentice, Carl Lowther. For doing the double, we won the Manny Mercer Trophy for the most stable points, which made me very proud.

This year, the two retiring old fogies, Peter Walwyn and I, were top-table guests of Len Cowburn, chairman of the boxing committee. I was asked to present the cup to the winner of the first bout, won by David Gregory, from Chris Thornton's yard, who beat Mark Lawson, who works for Henry Candy. The evening raised forty-five thousand pounds for the Stable Lads' Welfare Trust. Two auction items and a collection raised five thousand seven hundred pounds for Scott Taylor, himself a stable lads' boxer for the last ten years, now fighting the toughest battle of his life. Harry Beeby conducted the auction, which raised thirty-six thousand pounds, and the silent auction raised just over eight thousand six hundred pounds for the cause. Twenty years ago this event raised in excess of a hundred thousand pounds (one year they even raffled a Rolls-Royce), which shows the way things have gone.

Today, 3 November, Alan and I have spent all afternoon with Ian Bolland, our accountant, discussing the forthcoming takeover.

174

It was nice to hear from Steve Simpson of the *Blackpool Gazette* that our stable lass, Rachel Hume, has been voted the Stable Hand of the Year in the Derby Awards. I put Rachel's name forward some months ago for the unselfishness and dedication she showed in Japan when Bolshoi fractured a leg before his race. Rachel had to stay in Japan, on her own, over Christmas and New Year, without a single day off. She did not complain once. Her love and loyalty to her horse were way beyond the call of duty and I am very proud of her award. I was lucky enough to be given the President's Trophy on the same card.

Rachel is not like the girl Steve, our farrier, told me about, whose horse got colic. The vet asked her to lead the filly down the road for a few minutes, to try to get the animal's bowels moving. When the girl arrived back, an eager vet said, 'Did she pass anything?'

'Yes,' said the girl.

'Oh good,' the vet replied.

'A tractor and the postman.'

Lots of reporters have been ringing up these past few days for my thoughts on retirement and so forth. We also had a slot on *Look Northwest*. Tonight, 4 November, Flash came into my office during evening stables to ask me if I would give him a reference to go on a training course, so he is obviously walking his box and feels like training. Flash has been our head-man for ten years, and a very good one at that. No doubt he will miss the boss a little bit when I go.

For a giggle, we gave him two references.

Today, Bonfire Night, Alastair Down wrote a double-page article about Jo and me in the *Racing Post*. No doubt plenty of *Racing Posts* will end up on the fire tonight. Alastair gave my Tenerife project a good mention. God, I hope something comes of that.

On our second last day of Flat racing, our two-year-old, Indian Music, won the nursery at Doncaster with Gary Carter on board, in desperately heavy going at the generous odds of 33–1 (50–1 on the Tote). It was the sixtieth winner we have trained for Robert Aird in ten years. After Elaine Aird had received the trophy, we were invited to have a drink with the chairman of the racecourse. We were halfway there when an announcement came over the loudspeaker, 'Would

November 1999

TO: WHOM IT MAY CONCERN

Tony McWilliams has been our Head-Man for the past ten years, and during this time I have found him to be a real tea-leaf. So much so, he would take the headcollar off a night-mare! In fact, we search him every night when he has finished work, as he has an awful habit of taking things home.

Mr McWilliams is very clothes conscious and turns up for work in jeans with trendy worn out knees and a very nice pair of wellingtons to ride out in. Tony is also a very good time-keeper. You can guarantee he is first out of the yard, every breakfast, lunch and tea time. Tony's nickname is 'Flash'. It has absolutely nothing to do with the way he dresses. He acquires the name for the speed he shows when he gets out of the way when any jobs need doing, and the turn of foot he possesses on a Friday as he sprints to the office to collect his wages.

Hope this reference suffices,

Yours faithfully,

Jack Berry

Flash's reference

Jack Berry or his representative come to the weighing-room.' I asked Alan to go and see what they wanted. You can guess which stipe was on duty. As you might expect, Captain Hibbert-Foy was making a bit of a meal of Indian Music's last run at Catterick, compared to his improved run today. If these people had ridden in races themselves, they would know that there is a big difference between Catterick's sharp course, with undulations that would not be out of place at a motor-bike scrambling circuit, and Doncaster, with its wide open, beautifully straight, flat track.

Doncaster – November 1999

When Alan told Captain Hibbert-Foy that Indian Music did not handle the sharp bends and undulations at Catterick, he was told: 'That fact should have been reported to the Catterick stewards.' If you were to ask every jockey after any race at Catterick, over any distance, on any going, Flat or jumping, they will tell you that twenty per cent of their horses don't handle the track. If Captain Hibbert-Foy did not know that, he should be in Chechnya sorting the war out.

In all our years of training we have had plenty of horses that have been overrated, that could have done with a tug and given a few easy races. I have always resisted the temptation. In fact, I have lost horses from the yard on account of it. Why Captain Hibbert-Foy needed to question my integrity over our second to last Flat runner of an unblemished thirty-year training career, I don't know. As for Indian Music's win, instead of allowing us to savour the moment, the unnecessary inquiry shows the man in his true colours. What a thoughtless little man he is. In any case, I doubt if I would have waited thirty years to have a coup!

Jo and I stayed overnight at Doncaster with Ken Ivory and his partner Valerie on the eve of quite an emotional day for us, our final runner on grass. At 11.30 we went to the racecourse where Chris and Antonia had arranged a box for the day and, with some of our other owners, sponsored the lady riders' race. No end of people were wishing Jo and me well and taking our photograph. In the box, a great time was being had by all. Then the time came for the race and disaster struck.

Beverley Kendall, who, along with her boyfriend Graham, had returned to the fold a few weeks before, having worked for Ann Swinbank for a short time, was riding Best of All in our sponsored race. Beverley was going nicely and getting into the race as planned when our filly was crossed, catching the heels of the horse in front. Best of All came a right cropper, giving Beverley an awful fall. As Bev wasn't moving, I got a lift down the track to the prostrate jockey, who was still unconscious but being admirably attended by the on-the-spot doctors and medical staff. Beverley was loaded into an ambulance and, with me riding shotgun, we sped off to hospital with sirens screaming and cars diving for cover to get out of the way as we shot through red lights – John Carroll would have loved it. Bev was taken into the resuscitation room for a head scan, various X-rays and other tests, then into intensive care. It was later decided that Bev should go to the Royal Hallasham Hospital in Sheffield. How sorry we felt for her dad, Bob, the Country and Western singer, who had to do a gig in Scotland that night, while his wife legged it to Sheffield. I wouldn't mind betting that Bob has sung better than he did that night. Dozens of folk rang over the weekend enquiring about Beverley, including Radio Lancashire and Radio Cumbria. Bev has received lots of flowers and cards and thankfully has started to come round. What a worry, so soon after Scott Taylor.

With all the lunches and dinners we have attended this year, it's a wonder I'm not looking like Billy Bunter. Monday night was our annual Laurel Dinner. We always have a great night and a bit of a singsong. Jo was presented with a bottle of champagne and some flowers. As you can see, I now have a star named after me, which thrills me to bits, thanks to Pat and Andrew Hoyle, the bosses of the Laurel Racing Club.

On Tuesday, 9 November, when we had finished working the horses, Jo and I went to Manchester's BBC Studios, where I had a slot on Radio 5 with Ian Payne, talking about my involvement with racing.

Universal Star Listing

This certifies that the Universal Star Listing hereby designates the star having the co-ordinates:

Auriga   6h19m59s +28°25'36"

the following name:

Jack Berry MBE

This name is permanently recorded in our listing, which will be published and copyrighted in our book to be deposited with the British Library.

I bear witness to this registration, with the official seal of the Universal Star Listing, as recorded on:

8 November

1999

Registrar   Millennium 2000

Celestial chart: Spring, showing signs of the zodiac, astrological instruments and the positions of stars, engraved by John Emslie (1813-75) (engraving)
Private Collection/Bridgeman Art Library, London

JB, you are a star!

Laurel Racing Club

Tel / Fax: (01772) 734313

Laurel Leisure Limited,
P.O. Box 198,
Preston, Lancs.
PR2 7ED

November 8th 1999

THE JACK BERRY RETIREMENT CELEBRATION MENU

"STARTING OUT" - THE COCKERHAM VENTURE

Smoked Salmon, Melon Fan, Egg Mayonnaise, Cottage Style Mushrooms, Rollmop
Herrings, Fruit Juices.

"IN THE SOUP" - WITH THE TAXMAN!

Autumn Vegetable Soup

"MAIN COURSE" - THE AYR GOLD CUP CONNECTION!

Roast Venison, Roast Beef, Roast Duckling, Roast Chicken, Poached Salmon,
Poached Halibut, Vegetable Lasagne. Roast & Creamed Potatoes, Selection of
Vegetables.

"SWEET MEMORIES" - OI OYSTON, PARIS HOUSE, LAUREL QUEEN, MIND GAMES ETC!

Homemade Fruit Tart, Sherry Trifle, Peach Melba, Pear Helene, Pineapple Meringue,
Ice Cream.

"TAKING THE BISCUIT" - THE MBE COURSE!

Assorted Cheese and Biscuits

FINAL COURSE - "IT'S OVER TO ALAN"!

Coffee/Tea, Mint Biscuits

19

A Legend in The North

Today, 12 November, David Nicholson has announced he is giving up training. David was a decent jockey who rode his first winner in 1955 on his father's Fairval at Chepstow and his last on What A Buck at Hereford in 1974. David became a very talented trainer whose first success was in 1969 at Warwick with Arctic Coral. Although David wasn't everyone's cup of tea, he was a very confident man, rooted in his ideas, and ten times out of nine, in his opinion, he was right. David and I have been friends all our racing lives. When I mentioned to him last year that I was going to retire, he told me he was not far off doing the same. Well, now he has gone and beaten me to it. It will be a sad day for many of us if he and Dinah, his other half, stop feeding us at their annual picnic in the car park at Royal Ascot, a treat which is always a highlight of the event. Many of us also have Dinah to thank for our beautiful shiny toppers. I hope his successor at Jackdaws Castle carries on the tradition of open days which David himself started and which has raised countless thousands for good causes.

On Sunday, 14 November, it was all happening at the yard. Laurel Racing Club came to take photographs of their horse at 11.00 a.m. At the same time, the Monkey Club partnership had a meeting in the next room. At 2.00 p.m. seventy people from the Ponies Association (UK) came to look round and hold a seminar. Most of the punters were horse- and pony-show people, hoping to become equine judges. They were quite critical of some of the horses that we brought into the indoor school for them to see. The lads who held them said afterwards what cheeky buggers they were. The judges liked Garnock Valley quite a bit.

182

They said that although he had wear on his joints and wasn't level on his rump, he might possibly be all right as a racehorse.

'Is he any good?' one of them asked.

'He has won fourteen races,' I said, 'including his last one in a field of twenty-seven at Newbury. In fact, he runs tomorrow at Southwell and he will take a bit of beating.' Though I doubt if there were many big punters present, we had a laugh or two, followed by a buffet, and a raffle in aid of Riding for the Disabled.

The next day, Caroline Mia of the BBC came to have a day with yours truly, to make up a one-hour radio programme for our local station to go out in the New Year. Caroline came at 6 o'clock in the morning to see Nevill and myself feed the horses, and to get a feel of things. She was a lovely girl who asked the right questions and enjoyed every minute of her job. Caroline recorded the horses eating their grub, the blacksmith hammering away shaping up shoes on his anvil, horses walking round the yard, blowing after their exercise on the gallops, and the noise made by the clippers, as Lynne Varey was whipping the hair off the yearlings. The nicest sound of all came after Robbo and Pat Robinson had brought their pal Bill Robinson down from the Talbot Inn with the remaining Martell jug to complete the set of eleven and in the comfort of our front room we all shouted home Garnock Valley on the Racing Channel as he won his race at Southwell.

All our yearling colts are ridden and cantering away now, and the fillies are being lunged and driven in strings. As we only have a few all-weather horses and jumpers now in, it's quite easy to nip off around mid-morning. Today, Tuesday, 16 November, my new sponsored Saab arrived. I had arranged to meet up with IJF almoner Elaine Wiles to visit Scott Taylor at Hunter's Moon Hospital in Newcastle and this gave me a good opportunity to try out my new wheels. Although Scott is now out of his coma, we are all concerned about the extent of his brain damage. He has taken huge strides along the road to recovery since last time I saw him. Mandy, his New Zealand speech therapist, held a sheet of paper up with the words yes and no written on it, and said to Scott, 'Is your name Scott Taylor? Are you a jockey? Are you a mechanic?' and so on. Holding up another sheet of paper with the alphabet printed large, she said to Scott, 'What is the first letter of your Christian name? – and your surname?' She then produced a bag of gadgets and pulled out a pen, spoon, scisssors and a comb and asked Scott to point to the first letter of each object. He did so correctly. Elaine and I were so chuffed. It is eleven weeks since the young jockey was injured. Let's just hope and pray that he keeps on improving.

People's kindness and generosity continue to be shown by the variety of fund-raising events held for Scott's benefit. The Southern jockeys have played their Northern colleagues at football. Jump jockeys Robert Thornton, Xavier Aizpuru and Richard Johnson have been sponsored to dye their hair. But the boot can still go on the other foot. The Flat jockeys had collected over three hundred pounds for Scott at a September meeting at Redcar in a bucket, which they handed over to the declarations clerk, Cyril Greenland. He put the money in his briefcase for safety but from there it was stolen and never recovered. What a cruel, callous act.

The following day at Doncaster Sales, we sold the three remaining Red-Shirt Brigade horses. Red Typhoon sold for nine thousand six hundred guineas, making a nice profit as she originally cost two thousand six hundred as a yearling and won a couple of races. Jo and I then went on to Derek Taylor's in Sheffield to pick up some more pictures for charity auctions; they have proved quite an earner for various good causes. One in particular, a landscape scene of Hexham racecourse, made two thousand two hundred pounds for the Scott Taylor Fund. Derek, whom I met for the first time, was a very proud retired Royal Navy man, even his car number plate ended with XRN.

On account of the problems with the French banning our beef, the new wine released today didn't get a lot of hype this year. For all that, we were invited by Ann Hartley to a Beaujolais Nouveau party, which was great. We drank plenty of wine and talked about racing, particularly the time and expense of travelling to and from race meetings. Every year it gets worse. So much so, with the roads grinding to a halt almost daily, we could see racing becoming more centralised in time. It only needs the likes of Stan Clarke or Trevor Hemmings, high-powered business-men, to reform racing along American lines. Trainers would work more

PHOTOGRAPH: ANNE GROSSICK

Paddy Farrell and JB at Moss Side open day 1997

from barns on or near the track, with many of the smaller courses done away with. I wouldn't laugh too much. It could happen.

The following night I was back in the BBC's Manchester studio along with rally driver Natalie Barrett from a link-up in London. We were the guests of Charles Lambert on the Friday show, *The Seagulls Follow the Trawler*, for a talk-in on the dangers in sport. On my return home at 10.10 p.m., I took a call from Eileen Farrell telling me that her father, Paddy, had collapsed and died of a heart attack. The next day, Sunday, I arranged to meet Sarah Yorke, another IJF almoner, at Wetherby races where she acts as a steward, and go on afterwards to visit Mary, Paddy's wife.

While at Wetherby, Sarah asked me if I would receive a cheque for two thousand five hundred pounds on behalf of the IJF; they were the proceeds of a dance that had been held at St Martin's School near Helmsley, organised by Belinda Dickinson and Jane Barge.

When Sarah and I arrived at Paddy's house, Mary was in bits, as you would imagine, but coping. The Farrells are a really nice, close-knit family, something like the Waltons on TV, and very supportive of each other. Their son Patrick was on his way back from India, but their two daughters, Geraldine and Eileen, along with the youngest son Christopher, complete with their partners and the four grandchildren, were all at the house. 1999 had been a miserable year for the Farrells. It wasn't that long ago that Paddy told me he would be glad to see the back of it and was looking forward so much to the Tenerife holiday in the spring.

At 9.45 a.m. next morning I again caught the train to London. Arriving early at Euston station, I sauntered off for a cup of tea and a bite to eat to kill some time before making my way to 42 Portman Square, racing's Old Bailey, not, thankfully, to be hauled over the coals for some kind of misdemeanour, but to attend an Injured Jockeys Fund meeting, along with almoners Elaine Wiles, Serena Oxley, Sarah Yorke and Sue Mills, plus secretary Martina Lemaire and the trustees. After the meeting we went on to the Goring Hotel for our annual supper and a friendly chat. The trustees had to take it in turns to tell a joke, which was great fun, but I better not put any of them in print, especially the one Peter Scudamore told. When Brough Scott mounted his bicycle to ride off home, we all gave him a big cheer outside the hotel.

I stayed overnight at the Goring, as I had a meeting with my publishers the following morning before heading back north to Preston station. It was pouring with rain when Jo picked me up to take me to Paddy's house. Paddy looked so relaxed and at peace with himself, all his recent pain and suffering had gone. Jo and I travelled with the family to Haxby for mass at the St Margaret Clitheroe Church, which was absolutely packed. The hymns were nice and bright. Father O'Neill, who was in charge, had been a good friend of Paddy's and said some lovely things about him. Then it was my turn to say a few words:

'By the size of the gathering here tonight, I don't have to tell you Paddy Farrell had many friends. When Paddy came over from Ireland in 1953, I was an apprentice at Charlie Hall's yard, where he and I worked together for eight years and were great mates. I had the privilege of enjoying many Sunday lunches with him and Mary when they first got married. They treated me as part of the family. I even went home with them to Ireland for holidays.

'Paddy was not only an excellent jockey, as his record proves, he was a legend in the North. A brilliant horseman and a very good judge of a horse, he rode such good animals as Stormhead, State Secret, Knightsbrook, O'Malley's Point and Glorious Days. And at Towton we had lots of glorious days. However, tragedy struck the great man in the 1964 Grand National, when he came to grief at The Chair on Border Flight, and was subsequently paralysed from the waist down.

'At the time Paddy had a wife and four young children to support. The old jockey was a real family man and a devoted Catholic. We Northerners were gutted that our hero wouldn't be able to ride or walk again. To do something constructive to help the family we jockeys went round with buckets collecting, in between races, at Wetherby. The punters and bookmakers were exceptionally generous. We followed suit at Southwell and other race meetings. The press gave the cause a favourable mention, and, as always when needed in racing, kind folk sent in many donations to the Paddy Farrell Appeal.

'In the same season, "Iron Man" Tim Brookshaw broke his back in a fall in a race over hurdles, also at Liverpool. In a matter of months we had two of the country's leading jockeys paralysed. Tim's name was added to Paddy's and the fund became the Farrell Brookshaw Appeal Fund. Those two injured jockeys caught the public's imagination. People from all walks of life were donating money to the appeal, which rose to such heights that trustees had to be appointed. This laid down the foundations for the present-day Injured Jockeys Fund.

Although Paddy had lots of success riding many winners over the years, he also suffered. But his suffering was not in vain. Thanks to Paddy, the Injured Jockeys Fund will go on helping injured jockeys and their families, whatever their needs, for the forseeable future. Therefore, you can say that Paddy has made history, and his name will go in the racing record books and remain there forever. Like old soldiers who fought in the war, we will remember him. In racing, we have professional jockeys and gentleman riders. Patrick Anthony Farrell was a great professional, and an even greater gentleman.'

During prayers, Father O'Neill said, 'Let us pray for Paddy. In silence, let's think our own thoughts of Paddy.' I could have thought many, but one that instantly came to mind was a story I mentioned in my first book, *It's Tougher at the Bottom*, without quite telling the whole story. Paddy, Percy Hinchcliffe and I were going to Manchester races. Paddy had a couple of rides. I was home on a forty-eight-hour pass from the army and Paddy had got me a spare ride in the first race, a novice hurdle. Percy, an ex-lad from Hall's (who also rode a few winners), was going for a run out with us. It was an awful foggy day as was often the case in those days. We were driving down the old Mountainess Road, before the M6 and the M62 motorways were built, with Paddy at the wheel. A car stupidly overtook us and crashed into a car travelling in the opposite direction, which in turn pushed the overtaking culprit back into us, damaging the driver's side of Paddy's car. Paddy broke his nose on the steering wheel, Percy hurt his knees, got a bang on the head and badly tore his trousers, for which I think he claimed off Paddy's insurers. Paddy's nose was absolutely puring blood and all Percy kept saying was, 'Look at my f*****g trousers!'

I was in the front dozing off when it happened and thankfully I was unhurt. A woman got out of the other car, with a broken ankle, holding a screaming baby with blood on its face. The woman was also crying, but she would keep walking about. I told her to sit back in the car as she was making her ankle worse. The driver, who I assumed to be her husband, couldn't handle it. He just walked about with his face in his hands, having been told by Paddy in no uncertain terms 'what a fecking eejit' he was. Paddy rarely swore, but on occasions he said 'fecking', which at times sounded like something much worse.

Someone arranged to get an ambulance for the lady and the baby. Paddy managed to drive his car to Barnsley Hospital, with Percy in it, to get his nose fixed, while I got a lift on to the races, arriving too late for my ride. That was forty-one years ago, and today, for the first time ever, I am going to let a skeleton out of the cupboard, a secret I have even kept from The Bride throughout thirty-seven years of marriage and one getting to know her. I messed myself! And what a job I had trying to flush my Y-fronts down the toilet next to the weighing-room. Racing was nearly over by the time I got cleaned up and continued my story with the boys in the weighing-room about the crash. Thankfully, Father O'Neill, who knew I was real friendly with Paddy, didn't ask me what my thoughts were. With him being a man of the cloth, I would have had to come clean and tell him.

It was nice to see so many of the old jockeys there in church, more than enough of us to be pall bearers and do the business. As the likes of myself, Pat Gullwell, Gerry Kelly, Dicky Curran, Lex Kelly and Jimmy Power have all got a bit rickety with wear and tear over the years, Mary probably told the funeral directors, 'Don't let that lot carry Paddy, they might drop him.' When we got back to the house it was great to have a bit of crack with the old jocks and lads that Paddy and I rode and worked with.

On Saturday, 27 November, Jo took me to Haydock Park to meet John Oaksey and from there John and I travelled together to Ireland for Paddy's funeral. Bill Whittle, the Haydock Park boss, very kindly presented Jo and me with two annual members' badges for the year 2000. We are grateful for that, as we want to continue to go racing and wouldn't like to have arguments with the gateman on the owners' and trainers' entrance. Lancashire comedian Bernard Manning tells a story which goes something like this. Owner Chris Brasher was having trouble getting into a racecorse, having left his owner's badge at home. The doorman said, 'Tha can't come in here without a badge, sir. It's more than my job is worth to let you in this entrance. Tha will have to go and see the manager. To get there, go out to the main road, turn right, follow the back of the stands, pass the car-park entrance, keep going right to the bottom, turn right again, fifty yards or so you will come to a green door which says manager's office. Knock on it and if the manager's not out on't course, he will fix thee up wi' a badge or let tha in.'

'How far is it to the manager's office?' asked Chris.

'About half to three quarters of a mile,' replied the doorman, who I think was a Yorkshireman.

'Oh, come on! I've got a runner in the first race. Let me in.' Grabbing a racecard off the table, Chris said, 'Look, there's my name, Chris Brasher, owner of Run Like The Clappers.'

'Ah, *the* Chris Brasher, the man who ran the four-minute mile?'

'Yes, yes,' said Chris, his face lighting up and grinning from ear to ear.

'Well, it won't take tha long then, will it?'

At the Posthouse Hotel at Dublin airport, over our meal, John and I had a good chat about various things. John is a very interesting man, and great company. On our way to retire for the night, we two old boys passed a crowded ballroom and peeped in to see scantly clad young things flat out rock 'n' rolling to Bill Haley's 'Rock Around The Clock'. But there wasn't much chance of John and me gate-crashing the party, although there was a time when I would have done, as I have always loved dancing and music, and I have missed many a good party through not being invited!

Paddy's church service was at eleven o'clock on Sunday morning at Grange Con, the village where he and I rode out at Paddy Slater's many years ago. After breakfast, John and I picked up our hired wheels and set off just before nine, knowing only the direction to make for. John pulled rank and voted I drive, while he rode shotgun and did the navigating (Natalie Barrett would have been proud of him). The house, when we had found our way there, brought back many memories. Mrs Farrell, Paddy's mum, had been a super baker and cook and I could recall sitting down for tea on my first ever visit, some forty-five years ago, when every single edible thing on that table had been made by her, including the butter and the jam. Even the milk came from their house cow.

The church was packed with people, including Grand National winning jockeys Eddie Harty, who rode Highland Wedding to victory in 1969, and Willie Robinson, who won on Team Spirit in 1964, the year Paddy got broke up. John Oaksey gave a very good address in church. The burial was at Ballinglass cemetery. Although it was pouring with rain, John and I reckoned there must have been three hundred people around the graveside. What a sad day, but I am glad to have been there to see my old pal off. Christopher, Paddy's son, put my tape *Off and Running* in his dad's coffin, as Paddy played 'The Jolly Farmer' from the tape a lot. Chris said that if anybody came to the house, his dad would say, 'Listen to Jack Berry.'

JB and Sam Hulme in their waistcoats

Out came my black tie again on Monday for the funeral of one of our owners, John (Sam) Hulme, who was only fifty-eight. A nicer man would be hard to find. Sam and I had some real flash 'horsey' waistcoats made for Royal Ascot last year (mine was to commemorate our treble the year before). We thought they were great. If Sam was looking down on the mourners, no doubt he smiled when he saw me in my waistcoat.

Sam was a great lover of the country, gifted with a lovely even temperment and a great sense of fun. It was typical that the collection went to a wildlife charitable trust and a hospital equally. The church of St Mary's and All Saints at Whitmore in Staffordshire isn't very big, but it was crammed full, with many people listening to the service relayed outside.

191

On the first day of December, Amlwch ran second in the handicap chase at Catterick. Straight after the race I kicked on for home as Les Pijnen, the cameraman from the Racing Channel, was to be there at six to film the Martell Grand National water jugs, which commemorated every year from the 1989 race won by Little Polveir to the 1999 winner, Bobbyjo. There is even a jug for the year the race was void. The jugs, kindly donated by Bill Robinson (landlord of the Talbot at Bishopton, Co. Durham), are going to be auctioned on the Racing Channel in aid of the Injured Jockeys Fund. During the filming, Aiden Holland pledged a thousand pounds to start them off. The collection ended up being bought for thirty-one thousand pounds by none other than Robert Hitchens in Jersey, the gentleman who gave the fund a million pounds earlier in the year.

The following day I caught the 7.57 a.m. train to London to met up with the Injured Jockeys Fund trustees – John Oaksey, Jeremy Richardson, Bob McCreery, John Smith, Bill Smith, Brough Scott, Peter Scudamore and Dick Saunders – for lunch at the Goring Hotel with the Queen Mum.

Also invited was David Mould, who rode over a hundred winners for Queen Elizabeth the Queen Mother, along with the legendary Voice of Racing, Sir Peter O'Sullevan. The Queen Mum was in great form, as usual.

What a charmer.

I was talking to her when David Mould chimes in, 'What do you think, ma'am, of young Jack here retiring?'

'Yes,'she said, 'I read about that. Seeing will be believing.'

I told her that I would like to spend a year or so making sure that everything goes well for Alan, then I might buy a few acres in Yorkshire with enough boxes to train half a dozen or so jumpers.

'Now you're talking,' she said.

I reminded her of her jump interests in the North with Ken Oliver. Perhaps when I get my little yard she may remember me and grace the place with a horse?

'You never know. You just never know,' said the great lady, who went on to say that she was pleased to see me still wearing my red

*Dick Saunders, George Goring, JB, Sir Peter O'Sullevan, Bill Smith, John Smith,
Bob McCreery, John Farley, Brough Scott, Peter Scudamore, Jeremy Richardson,
David Mould, QM, Lord Oaksey*

shirts. We had an excellent lunch which I am sure she enjoyed. We certainly all did.

Ian Bolland, our accountant, likes to take the mickey out of me about my special liking for these occasions. He has invented a myth that, hearing of my impending retirement, the Queen Mother visited the yard and I was showing her round the stables when a two-year-old nearby let go with a resounding fart that registered eight on the Richter Scale. It rattled the windows and frightened the dogs and I just could not ignore it.

'Oh dear,' said I to the Queen Mum, 'I am frightfully sorry about that.'

'Think nothing of it, Jack,' she said, 'actually, I thought it was one of the horses.'

Within half an hour of getting home, Liz Wharton rang to say that her mother had died. The number of funerals that I have attended this year seems unreal.

On Friday, Ian Bolland spent most of the day at our yard. Three different bank managers came at staggered times to sort out the finances for Alan's takeover. In the evening, Jo and I went to the Over-60s' Christmas party – and what a good do it was too! Our yard is a mile and a half outside the village of Cockerham. When we are not on the road, we are working at home, which explains why, strange as it must seem, I don't know the names of a dozen people that live in our village. It's nice to go to local functions when we can so that the locals can see the pair of us, instead of just reading about us in the papers.

20

The Final Curtain

Saturday, 4 December 1999. This day last year I announced, at our end-of-season party, my intention to retire and hand over the reins to Alan. In three weeks time that becomes official. At the moment, I have no regrets. I suspect I will probably miss the racing less than working with the horses, especially the yearlings. I will continue to go racing but, ideally, I would love to buy a nice house with a few acres in Yorkshire and get back to my roots. Living in Lancashire with some of our neighbours, one sometimes gets the feeling that the Wars of the Roses are not quite over. For all that, we have had some wonderful times at Cockerham and I will always love the place.

I have often been asked which is the best horse we have trained. It's a hard question to answer as – fortunately – we have been graced with some real good horses. Bri-Eden, who won the Group 3 Ballyhogan Stakes in 1983, was, I believe, the first gelding to win a Group race. O. I. Oyston won twenty-four races and is still here at the grand old age of twenty-four next month. Laurel Queen was the most prolific winning filly or mare since the war, with twenty-four British wins to her credit. Palacegate Touch has won the most individual races for us, with a score of twenty-seven. If and when we finally find a place, we will probably set up an old codgers' home for retired racehorses, as I intend to take Olly with me, and of course Palacegate Jack, Palacegate Touch (Archie), Ansellman (Marco), Garnock Valley (Garny) and Amron (Ronnie) will want to come as well. Two other old-stagers, Bolshoi and Selhurstpark Flyer (George), have got reserved boxes at their owners' studs to retire to.

Bri-Eden, Mind Games, Paris House, Distinctly North, Bolshoi, Selhurstpark Flyer, Palacegate Episode, Lucky Parkes, Rosselli and

195

Another Episode have got to be the best horses that we have had the pleasure of training on the Flat. Also worthy of a mention are Clantime, I Don't Mind, Touch Boy, Area Code, Almost Blue, Sky Royal, Donovan Rose, Dancing Music, Amron, Our Fan, Boozy, Lindseylee, Hong Kong Girl, Dream Talk, Tod, Croft Imperial, It's All Academic, Prohibition, Gorinsky, Food Of Love, Great Chaddington, Amber Mill, Sharp Anne, Valdermosa, Cee-Jay-Ay, Doublova, Laurel Queen, Sizzling Saga, Heaven-Leigh-Grey, Regal Quest, Diamond Mine, Whittingham, Snowgirl, Bit-A-Magic, Fylde Flyer, Nifty Fifty, Mammas Too, Sabre Rattler, Laurel Delight, Palacegate Touch, Margaret's Gift, Garnock Valley, Tuscan Dawn, Palacegate Jack, Never In The Red, Very Dicey, Lago Di Varano, Limerick Belle, Persian Fayre, Up And At 'Em, Best Of All, Ansellman, My Melody Parkes, O. I. Oyston, Albert The Bear, For Old Times' Sake, Limerick Princess, Olympic Spirit, Speedy James, Young Bigwig, Salamanca, Tuscan Dream, Eastern Lyric, Iris May, Just Another Time, Queensland Star, Angie Baby, Lunch Party, Kastaway, Ace of Parkes, Cartmel Park, Zaragossa, Bon Ami, Singsong, Brave Burt, Glenrock and Susie's Flyer.

For those of you with good memories, we trained the jumpers Duffle Coat, New City, Red Earl, Glenzier Lad, Bold Warrior, Solares, Canobie Key and Kas. More recently, Amlwch, Smolensk and Carlisle Banditos have also done well over fences. When we get settled into our next, and we would like to think our last, place (Jo and I do not want to be chasing around like gypsies), it would be good to see a few chasers going round trained by J.Berry.

To make a change from the village hall, this year we held our final end-of-season party at the Garstang Country Hotel and Golf Club. Adrian Ross was again the master of ceremonies and did the disco. We had a good turnout, including a few of our ex-lads and lasses, which is always nice to see. It was also good to see Beverley at the party. Graham, her boyfriend, managed to get her out of hospital for a couple of hours. Bev is recovering well after losing her memory and co-ordination for a while. She is in Sharoe Green's young disabled persons' unit at Preston, the same hospital that our Sam was in 1985 when he got hurt. When Jo and I went to see Bev, it was like old times.

The cake

Some of the same staff and patients are still there after fourteen years, including Bernard Robinson, Beverley Curtis and Aisha Hajat, who were so pleased to see us. We should spare a thought for these people when we moan about trivialities, as we aften do. One of the nurses was

197

telling me that the mini-bus bought from the proceeds of one of our open days finally came to the end of its tether and was replaced last year by a new one, given by the Lords Taverners.

Our owners came to the party from as far away as Ireland and from all parts of Britain. Helen and Sue, from our office, made a great job of decorating the hotel function room – in red, white and blue, of course. Lyn Campion made Jo and me a beautiful fruit cake, even iced in our colours.

John Conway gave us a bedside lamp in the shape of a shirt, no marks for guessing the colour. John Carroll rang up from Dubai to wish us well and said he missed being with us at the party, which was nice. The hotel manager came up to me just as I was about to make my speech, saying: 'Mr Berry, I am so sorry to interrupt you again but I have just received another phonecall for you, which the gentleman who rang said was very important. Please ring this number asap. It's urgent.' As I had my mobile with me (to get a commentary from Wolverhampton where Dance Little Lady finished fourth), I rang the number which the manager had given me, fearing the worst, only to hear a recorded message which said, 'This is the Cambridge Lesbian Line . . . ' That's the kind of trick John Carroll plays, but I don't think that it was him tonight.

Chris Deuters then got up and said some nice things about Jo and me, after which our staff presented us with a lovely plate (again in our colours) to commemorate our retirement, a bottle of bubbly and a bunch of flowers for Jo. It was really moving. Adrian then announced that I was going to say a few words and this is how they went:

'Welcome, everybody, to our end-of-season party. It doesn't seem a year since I stood on the stage at Cockerham, telling you that I was going to retire, and that this would be my last season as trainer.

'My year is up in three weeks' time, then Alan is the new master, although I will be helping out as understudy for a little while. Whenever he wants me to saddle up a runner, I will be there.

'But if he thinks I'm going to Wolverhampton in the middle of winter on a Saturday night, he can think again!

'To be honest, this season hasn't been the best that we have had –

though we shouldn't grumble too much, as we have still trained seventy-two winners and finished around eighth numerically from about four hundred trainers with full Flat licences in the trainers' list. In view of that you could hardly say that I have failed. However, I will go down as the trainer who didn't train a Group 1 winner, so I failed on that score. That's tough. However, we will go down in the same books as training the Ayr Gold Cup winner in 1988, and that was the winner I set out to train even before I had a licence.

'Since our first winner, Camasco, on the 16 December 1969, in the Earston Selling Hurdle at Kelso, exactly thirty years ago, we have had the privilege of training the winners of fourteen hundred and eighty-two races on the Flat in Britain and sixteen hundred and fifty-seven in all, with winners abroad and jumpers. From selling hurdle winners to Group 2, we have trained for some lovely people, and some right prats. From prison warders to High Court judges, they have helped the yard to get winners. I thank you all, past and present owners, most sincerely, and our stable staff for looking after the horses.

'We have some very nice yearlings in for next season, along with some decent three-year-olds and older horses for Alan to train. I hope he can do something that I didn't do and train a Group 1 winner. When he does, if it gives him as much pleasure and satisfaction as Albert gave Jo and me when he won the Ayr Gold Cup, I can tell you, it will be some feeling.

'Throughout the years we have had some great days. Jo and I have hundreds of photographs and cuttings in scrapbooks which I have stashed away and purposely haven't loked at. In our old age, we will get them out. Picture the scene:

'"Do you remember him when he won at Beverley?"

'"No, Jo. It wasn't Beverley, it was Bath."

'"Well, I knew it began with a B."

'We may very well lapse into dementia, but before that frightful day arrives, Jo and I possess a wonderful fund of memories and a lot of you figure in them. As I have said before, thank you all for the fun and for whatever part you played in getting the winners for the Moss Side Racing outfit, and indeed at Arksey beforehand.

JB cuts the cake with Jo

'May I ask you all to raise your glasses to the future of the horses, the owners, the staff and Alan. If the occasion arises where Jo and I can be of any help, we are only a phonecall away. Thank you all for the past and good luck for the future. Jo and I have had lots of pleasure training the winners over the years and we hope to have a lot more watching Alan training them now.

'Like it or not, for probably the last time ever (unless Alan does it next year), Adrian, let's have it – "The Jolly Farmer".'

Thank you for taking the time to read my book. I hope that you enjoyed it.